NEVER GIVE UP

NEVER GIVE UP

Memoirs
by Mary Saran

Foreword by Sir Arthur Lewis

OSWALD WOLFF

LONDON

First published by
Oswald Wolff (Publishers) Ltd, London
1976

ISBN 0 85496 257 3

Made and printed in Great Britain by
The Whitefriars Press Ltd, London and Tonbridge

Contents

v

Acknowledgements

In writing her memoirs during the last three years of her life—she died at seventy-eight on 16 February 1976, four weeks after the manuscript went to press—my mother received help from many people, most of whom it is not possible to mention individually here. My husband and other members of the extended family and friends in Britain, Germany and farther afield gave her encouragement and comments on early drafts which she found most helpful when preparing the final manuscript.

On style my mother would have wished to acknowledge the assistance she received from Vera Adamson, an old friend from the Hampstead days, who helped prepare the manuscript for publication. Sue Hogg and Doris Quinn read the proofs, and this welcome help, so soon after my mother's death, I should like to acknowledge.

London, 1 April 1976

Rene Saran

Abbreviations

Bewag   *Berliner Elektrizitätswerke Aktien-Gesellschaft* (Berlin Electricity Works Limited)

CIVIC   Council for the Investigation of Vatican Influence and Censorship

Gestapo   *Geheime Staatspolizei* (Secret State Police)

ICSDW   International Council of Social Democratic Women

IJB   *Internationaler Jugendbund* (International League of Youth)

ILP   Independent Labour Party

ISK   *Internationaler Sozialistischer Kampfbund* (Militant Socialist International)

KPD   *Kommunistische Partei Deutschlands* (German Communist Party)

NGO   Non-governmental Organisation (within the UN)

SA   *Sturmabteilung* (Stormtroops)

SC   *Socialist Commentary*

SPD   *Sozialdemokratische Partei Deutschlands* (Social Democratic Party of Germany)

TUC   Trades Union Congress

UN   United Nations

UNESCO   United Nations Educational, Scientific and Cultural Organisation

USPD   *Unabhängige Sozialdemokratische Partei Deutschlands* (Independent Social Democratic Party of Germany)

Foreword

Mary Saran lived her whole life in the socialist cause, as organiser, lecturer, writer and editor; first in Germany, then in Britain and ultimately in the international socialist movement. It was a rich life, both for her and for all those who came into contact with her, to be influenced by the integrity, devotion to the cause, and capacity for friendship which radiated from her. But it was also a life of frustrations, because of the terrible times through which we have been passing, so we must also hail her steadfast courage.

Perhaps the most cheering time to have been born a socialist in Europe would have been around the year 1830. One would have grown up in a time of turbulence, maturing during the Hungry Forties and the revolutions culminating in 1848; and the ideals then etched into one's soul would never be erased. (The 1930s would affect young socialists in the same way.) Then after 1850 one would live through enormous progress for the working classes, until about 1900, including rising standards of living, better health and education, the franchise, the strengthening of civil liberties, the rise of trade unions and so on. One could then die happily in 1900 convinced that the human race was essentially good, and that paradise was just around the corner.

The least cheering time to be born was when Mary was born, in 1897. Prices had just begun their long twenty-five year climb, at the expense of wages, which would see the trade union movement locked in the bitter industrial struggles of the Edwardian era. The Great War would follow; then the dislocation of the twenties, the Great Depression of the 1930s, Hitler, the Second World War, and the dislocation and famine which continued until around 1950. For Mary to have lived through all this without losing her faith in humanity is itself an achievement.

For socialists one of the worst consequences of this turbulent half century was the splitting of the movement into two sections, a totalitarian and a democratic section. The totalitarians detested the democrats, and wherever they came to power gave first priority to "liquidating" social democrats. We, for our part, have denied their right to call themselves

socialists, since both their denial of civil rights and their élitism are
anathema to us.

The split is troublesome to both sides, since it menaces the internal
cohesion of each. They are continually troubled by "subversives", who
wish to shed the totalitarian skin, while the democratic movement is torn
between the statist and the anarchist traditions of socialism. Its "left"
wing flirts with the communists, while its "right" wing hopes to convert
and capture the vote which grew up as liberal-radical.

Mary's lasting contribution to this period was her editorship of *Socialist
Commentary* and its predecessor *Socialist Vanguard*. In the 1940s and
1950s the other two journals of British socialism were both of the "left".
Socialist Commentary became the journal of the "right", especially after
Hugh Gaitskell lent it his name. The journal was produced exclusively by
love. Mary and then Mary and Rita Hinden built up a stable of unpaid
writers of the social democratic tradition. In those days the centre of
gravity of the British trade union movement was slightly right of centre of
the Labour Party so, if heads were to be counted, *Socialist Commentary*
was the movement's most representative mouth-piece. Its circulation grew
rapidly, and it was unsurpassed for the quality of its contributions.

From her editorship Mary moved into the office of the international
socialist movement, and soon began to cultivate especially relations with
women's movements in the so-called Third World. In that world
democratic socialism is sown on stony ground. Nearly all its self-styled
socialist leaders are authoritarian and élitist (though not necessarily
totalitarian) and our best hope is that they may learn from Djilas and Mao
Tse Tung that participation is central to the socialist mode. Work for
women's rights makes a little more progress because most modernisers pay
at least lip-service to the equality of women; but there is a long road to
travel. Mary played a noble part in arranging support for training women
from the Third World for community development work, especially in
relation to women's needs and organisations.

It is important to any movement to record the lives of those who have
kept it going through trying times. Towards the end of the 1960s
Americans around the age of twenty were earning themselves the title of
"the generation without heroes". Asked whom they admired, past or
present, they could think only of others of their own age group. My
generation was proud of belonging to a long tradition, and could reel off
hundreds of names, past and present, political and non-political, to whose
lives we admitted our debt. It is terrible to grow up without having anyone
to admire; this is fertile ground for cynicism and psychopathy. This record
of Mary's life is valuable not only for those of us who have known her, but

also for all its other readers, because it shows a gentle spirit, called to work for the cause of humanity, and holding fast to its calling through every tribulation.

Princeton, March 1976   W. Arthur Lewis

Introduction

The idea that I might write my memoirs has pursued me for some time. I have lived a full and interesting life and participated in important events. It is tempting to examine the factors which influenced my development and to recall the part I played in these events.

Born in 1897, I spent the years of my childhood and early youth during the prosperous era of Imperial Germany. Its long spell of peace, however, was approaching its end. When the First World War broke out, I had just reached the age of seventeen. By the time the war was over my basic convictions and the main direction of my life were clear. The hectic fifteen years of the Weimar Republic which followed were overshadowed by the restoration of the reactionary forces, the decline of democracy, the economic crisis, the rise of Hitler, the Labour movement's failure to resist it, and, finally, the growing threat of another world war. Hitler's triumph in 1933 forced me into political exile, and I found refuge in Britain. After the Second World War I did not return to Germany. By that time I was a British citizen and so was my daughter; Britain had become home for us. But the sphere of my interests widened beyond Britain and, gradually, beyond Europe, as I became increasingly active within a broader international framework. Retirement in 1963 at the age of sixty-six from the positions I had held in the Socialist International for thirteen years did not end my active participation in public work; my opportunities for world-wide travel in the cause of my self-chosen missions even increased.

My life has been enriched by the chances I have had of making friends in many parts of the globe. My roots are in Europe, including Britain, but I have also come to feel like a world citizen.

PART ONE

I

Childhood and Youth in Imperial Germany

Memories of my childhood were recently revived when I read the diary kept by my father for nearly forty years; I had not known of its existence before. Following the custom of recording family events, father started the diary in 1880, soon after he had married; with several longer intervals he continued it until the end of the First World War. After my own mother's death (she was his second wife) in 1919 he made no further entries. Although he lived for a few more years, with one daughter or another keeping house for him, he probably felt very lonely. His personal life had centred on mother, who had been a tower of strength to him ever since she had married the widower with three children, her elder by fifteen years. Father's first wife had hanged herself in an attack of melancholy of which he seems to have noticed no signs previously. The discovery of her suicide must have come as a deep shock to him. But of this his diary says nothing. He simply wrote: "My dear Käte died".

Mother died of cancer. Her death was unexpected; father had always thought that he would be the first to go. He did not only suffer a great personal loss. He felt lost, too, in the changed post-war situation to which he was unable to adjust. His whole world with its established values collapsed with the overthrow of the Hohenzollern Monarchy in Germany. Though not yet due for retirement, he at once resigned from his civil service post in the Ministry of Public Works. He had a strong sense of honour, linked with a kind of feudal allegiance. "I have sworn an oath of loyalty to the Kaiser," I remember him saying, "I am too old to serve the Republic now".

I was ten years old when we moved to Berlin. Before I had lived for five years at Königsberg in East Prussia, and another five years at Wiesbaden in the Rhineland. My childhood was a happy one. I was number seven in a family of altogether ten children. We formed three groups, divided by gaps of several years: three were from father's first wife, two boys and a girl; my mother had four girls in quick succession of whom I was the youngest; then came one boy and again two girls. In having seven children mother followed in the footsteps of her own mother. Her two sisters and four brothers, on the other hand, had no more than two, three or four children, and one had none at all. On father's side there were two sisters; only the younger one had children, five girls. Still, the close family circle was fairly large.

Father's income was modest. German government officials did not earn much in those years even after reaching higher positions. We had enough room in house and garden or surrounding spaces. As a matter of course, there were domestic servants, first two, then only one when my elder sisters left school and became what was called "house-daughters", at least for a number of years. But less was spent on food and clothes, or on furniture and equipment, than was customary in families of our acquaintances. When we had children's parties in our home, we pleaded in vain for a dessert (usual elsewhere) in addition to sandwiches and fruit juice. Nor were we any luckier with our protests against the black aprons we had to wear at school. They were useful in hiding ink spots and making dresses last longer, but they were ugly, and others were wearing gay coloured ones or none at all. Like most children we disliked being different from our fellows. However, our parents did not believe in spoiling us. Most of the time our coats and dresses were inherited from the older ones or better-off relatives. When at fourteen I suddenly grew taller than any of my older sisters, I was pleased that I could claim new dresses.

Mother set an example by dressing with the greatest simplicity herself. Throughout my childhood I remember her having two silk dresses to wear in turn at any of the official occasions she had to attend, one golden-brown, the other bluish-grey. Father's only luxury was his well-stocked wine cellar—his father, after all, had owned a wine bar at Magdeburg. My parents' modest form of recreation was towards the evening to cycle to the nearby *Grunewald*. But they found the money to send us children to swimming lessons, to skating (how I loved skating on the frozen lakes around Berlin) and to the theatre performances for which the school provided cheap tickets.

Our parents were not ostentatiously affectionate, but we were aware of their love and care, within a firmly established framework of discipline and, from early on, obligations to lend a hand in house and garden and with the younger children. We enjoyed a healthy measure of freedom to play (companions being available at all times) and scope to develop independently. Käte, for example, when only fifteen, was entrusted with the care of the six children younger than herself when the family moved from Wiesbaden to Berlin, and these seven youngsters were sent to our grandparents at Minden until the furniture arrived in Berlin. We even had to change trains, but thought nothing of it. The only incident on that journey was that one beret fell out of the window. We could not face arriving with one of us lacking headgear, so the youngest got one made out of a handkerchief, and all berets moved up until the bereft girl was reached. We had great fun at stations, lining up behind the window, proud of succeeding in keeping other passengers away from our compartment.

At home we were never bored. On winter evenings we usually sat around the table in the living room by an oil lamp—we had electricity but oil was cheaper. On Sundays mother used to read stories to the smaller ones, illustrated by pictures, on themes from the Bible. To those who stayed up after supper father would read books. One of his favourite authors was Fritz Reuter, a humorist of a somewhat radical persuasion who in the 1848 revolution had been imprisoned in a fortress. This author's biting social criticism did not exactly accord with our parents' basic outlook on life and society, but father appreciated his earthy humour. One winter father taught us Italian, a language he loved; we learned enough to enjoy parts of the famous novel by Alessandro Manzoni, *The Betrothed, a Tale of Seventeenth Century Milan.* When some of us could play instruments, there were musical evenings with cousins or friends joining in. I acquired a love of classical music, even though I did not get far with my own piano lessons. However, I persevered for several years. It was part of a middle-class girl's education to learn to play the piano, and I hesitated to plead for discontinuation because I thought that our piano teacher needed the money. We pitied her in any case since she had lost her hair and had to wear a wig—something rare and embarrassing at that time. When we were older, there was an "open" Sunday at our home once a month during the winter when young friends came as they wished, and we played games, sometimes even danced, although mother tried to avoid the latter.

School did not play a major part in my life, nor did my home work bother me until my late teens when *Abitur* approached, i.e. the university entrance examination at the end of grammar school. During the war, with the younger teachers away in the army, many lessons were boring. But I developed techniques of hiding from the eyes of the teacher the interesting books I was surreptitiously reading. I do not remember any revolts against authoritarian methods used at school. With some friends I enjoyed engaging in a mild form of passive resistance when every morning we put on some fantastic headgear made of any old cloth, and dashed past the teacher who was watching outside the school entrance for the "hatless". We felt like pioneers of the hatless fashion just coming in.

However, a characteristic incident may illustrate the situation. It occurred in my earlier school years at a private girls' school in the Berlin suburb of Lichterfelde. One of my class mates was Gertrud Strelewicz, who later became known as an actress. She infected many of us with her enthusiasm for the theatre, and, under her direction, we often acted scenes in intervals in a courtyard hidden behind the school building (a forbidden place). For a patriotic occasion (probably the Kaiser's birthday) she was selected to recite a poem. She was delighted because she loved reciting. But suddenly this was called off, without any reason being given. We discovered the reason: it had transpired that her father was an atheist.

In the earlier years of father's career, with our rapidly growing family, it was not easy for my parents to make ends meet. Father was able to earn something on the side as an architect, which helped to finance family festivities and the travel on which our parents were keen. In fact, they ventured farther than was usual in those days, to Italy, Turkey, Russia. The detailed descriptions in father's diary of their travel inside and outside Germany reflect the pleasure they derived therefrom. The children's interests in nature, walking and travel were encouraged, and we all retained these interests in later life. Holidays with relatives or friends took us to different parts of Germany. Once our parents with seven of their children (we had saved for this for several years) spent a month's holiday at the seaside, at Cranz in East Prussia which is now part of Soviet Russia, the place of my birth (mother then had spent the summer there to escape from the sticky heat of Königsberg where we lived).

My parents were happiest with small children. They welcomed unreservedly each new arrival in the family, and would undoubtedly have abhorred the idea of family planning had it been put to them. When an aunt died in childbed, with her husband away in the war, mother at once took a train to fetch the newborn baby and the two older children. This was characteristic of her for she was always ready to help, often going to the limit of her strength, but she was also seizing the chance of having another batch of small children at home. Father's entry in the diary reads: "We old people enjoy having small children again".

Often, when our parents went on one of their journeys, they placed us children in different families. On one such occasion, father proudly remarked: "And if we had even more little girls to board out, we would have found plenty of families ready to welcome them". He seemed sure that we would always behave well! Father's diary notes show his awareness of the fact that, as we became teenagers, our parents lost their grip on us. Once he sadly recorded that the four girls of the middle group preferred their own company to that of their parents. I was the youngest of these four—Käte, Lucie, Hilde, Maria—and insisted on belonging to this group rather than being left with the younger ones, which was so much less exciting. We sometimes had our little quarrels, but on the whole we experienced the usual solidarity in relation to parents and other adults. Käte, with her imaginative nature, was our leader in games which she knew how to make interesting. Lucie was the most selfless one, always quietly and cheerfully taking upon herself duties neglected by any of the others. With Hilde I lived for some time in a state of tension over small controversies, for instance, how to arrange things in the room we shared. Yet later we were very close, and remained so for life. I chaperoned her, discreetly disappearing for hours, when her love affair with her future husband was becoming serious. It was expected of me, the grammar school girl, that I would help the younger three with their home work. This often annoyed me—had not we, the older ones, always had to manage on our own? With Elisabeth and Inge, the two youngest, the task was not too burdensome. But with Ernst-Richard, it was hell. For he was a psychopath, really beyond help. There were early signs of this which I remember. He would steal, but not bother to remove or hide the evidence. He lacked a sense of prudence as well as moral inhibitions. It was never considered that he was in need of psychiatric treatment. Poor mother merely tormented herself by asking where she had failed with this tall, handsome boy, her only son. Evidently, my parents' knowledge of psychological questions was minimal.

Mother did not live to see what finally happened to her son when the turmoils of the post-war years caught up with him. Towards the end of the war he was sent, at considerable expense, to a boarding school in the Rhineland, such a school being the last resort of middle-class parents unable to cope with their teenagers. In 1918 the Rhineland was occupied by the victorious allied troops, and the school was closed. Ernst-Richard became engaged in dubious trading deals with allied soldiers. Later he volunteered for the "frontier guards" in the east, a kind of para-military corps in which early Nazi types assembled. Ernst-Richard was one of the first to join a Nazi Party unit. His membership card, as I learned later, bore such a low number that he would have been able to claim a high post under the Nazi régime had he returned from Canada after 1933. As it was, he never returned. The family had sent him there, after an attempt to provide a training for agricultural work, in the hope that, by being forced to work, he might find his way in the vast North American Continent. Gradually, all trace of him was lost.

Father's first wife had committed suicide in an attack of melancholy. Yet when in two of her children signs of melancholy appeared, they went unnoticed for quite a time. Walter's difficulties were due to fears and embarrassment when he had shirked an examination. Fortunately, the shadows which this cast over our home were soon dissipated. Not so in Grete's case, which shook me deeply. She was facing problems in her marriage. Her baby was born at our house, since her husband was serving in the army. Suddenly, she turned away from the baby and did not want to have anything to do with it. Just then she had learned, for the first time and by chance, of her mother's suicide, and began to talk about wanting to end her own life. My parents were away for a cure, and we, her sisters, had to cope. We did not want to call our parents back early. But how relieved we were when they returned.

There was a further complication. Grete's husband was a Catholic whose mother insisted on the baby being baptised as a Catholic. Grete was not over-concerned about this, although she would have preferred her children to be brought up in the Protestant religion, to which she adhered. She had an easy-going nature and would accept compromises, even sacrifices, for the sake of harmony in her marriage. But she must have felt how deeply hurt my parents were, especially mother whose faith was more rigid. I remember the day when we all went to the Catholic church where the baby was baptised. Mother's face looked icy and hostile; she could hardly control her sorrow.

This was my first personal experience of the deep divisions caused by denominational differences and of the tragedies resulting from dogmatic adherence to religious beliefs. Catholicism, as I saw it then, was a source of great intolerance. But my own struggle, which by then was in its initial stages, was with the Protestant variety of the Christian faith, into which I happened to have been born.

Another crisis in our family had occurred before the First World War, marking the end of our more carefree days at home. This concerned my sister Käte. On father's return from an official visit to the United States of America, he was received with the news that Käte, then at home as "house-daughter", was expecting an illegitimate child by a young man, hardly out of school, who had been a frequent, welcome visitor to our home. Father's diary entries show his emotional upset. He departed from his usual reticent way of referring to unpleasant or sad events. "Shame", "dishonour", "betrayal of our trust", "frivolity", the "disgusting need to hide things from society"—in terms like these, he recorded what had happened. What made things worse was that marriage, the only "honourable" way out, was impossible; the young lover had shot himself. If he had married Käte, he would have had to abandon his army officer's career, for neither of them had money, and an officer in the Imperial army depended on that. I believe that the strongest motive for his suicide was a feeling of utter helplessness. He could see no solution and was too immature to seek advice from people who might have helped. He knew, too, that his father, also an army officer, would be immensely disappointed, and he could not face this. My parents thought it was their duty to inform the young man's father when Käte's boy was born; it must have been a difficult letter to write. There was never any reply.

At sixteen, I did not see the full social implications of this individual tragedy. But I was deeply disturbed by the experience of prejudice and outworn caste tradition destroying one young life and harming another. When, on the fatal day, Hilde broke the news to me, and added that "now we must realise that *our* chances of marriage have gone", I remember smiling inwardly. Surely, she exaggerated. It seemed too ridiculous that even we, the innocent sisters, should be considered beneath the standards of respectable society. The thesis of "guilt by association" never appealed to me.

My parents blamed the man, the seducer, rather than their daughter. He had left her to face the consequences alone; this, in father's words, was the "greater of his crimes". I know that for mother, as for many women of her generation, sex was an obligation to be accepted, or even endured, with marriage. She had no understanding of the power of passions which could move man and woman equally. Of sex education, not suprisingly, she knew nothing. Both these young people were unprepared for their experience, and this was not unusual.

Be that as it may, in the event, my parents gave Käte every possible support. Her chances of marriage were now diminished, so everybody believed. Thus the need for her to have a profession was recognised. As soon as possible she started a training for baby care work. Later she specialised in maternity care. In this profession it was reckoned, as in that of midwife, she could call herself "Mrs", whether married or not. It would therefore be easier to live with an illegitimate child. Meanwhile, when the boy was a few months old, mother brought him into our home; she could no longer stand him being with a foster mother. "He needs a *real* home," she said apologetically when she suddenly appeared with the baby in her arms. Awkward questions had to be faced. Mother would meet them with a brief "he is an unfortunate orphan," and her face was such as to deter further questions.

My parents acted in a humane manner, and I respected them for their courage in defying a widely held prejudice. It was certainly not easy at that time. Not long afterwards, the war broke out, which made the situation less difficult as it brought other matters to the fore.

When Käte got married after all, she took her boy into her own home. Her husband agreed to adopt him legally. He was a good man, I understand. I only met him once because I broke the links with nearly all members of my family when I began to go my own way, and became totally absorbed in a desperate political struggle.

Many years later, I began to think of Käte again. She had become an ardent Nazi activist, while I, a refugee from Nazi persecution, lived in Britain and reflected a great deal about the causes of Hitler's triumph. This was the subject on which I addressed innumerable meetings all over the United Kingdom between 1933 and 1939. I used to trace the German disaster to the economic crisis with its millions of unemployed, the support Hitler received from industrialists, the weakness of the Weimar Republic and the disunity of the Labour movement. I admitted that the Versailles Treaty was an aggravating factor, but, in my view, not a decisive one. All these circumstances have since been fully explored in books written by Germans and non-Germans alike. But one psychological question has perhaps not yet been adequately resolved in many minds: even if, strictly speaking, Hitler was not elected by a majority of the people and did not come to power in a constitutional way, how could so many people have fallen for such an evil régime?

In trying to answer this question, I also thought of members of the family from which I came, personally kind and decent people, not victims of the run-away inflation of the early twenties, not economically desperate, yet joining or supporting the Nazis, even though many of them did not work so enthusiastically for Hitler as Käte did. There are many explanations, some of which are also relevant to other countries with terror régimes where the same question arises. In connection with Käte's story, I glimpsed one aspect of the situation which showed how complex it was.

For her personally, the Nazi movement had a liberating effect. The frustrations and humiliations to which she had been subjected in her youth had lingered on, although outwardly she had been able to cope with life. When the Nazi ideas swept over Germany these early experiences were at last washed away. In Nazi eyes, merely as a mother of sons (she had three) Käte was a person to be highly esteemed. Moreover, as a group leader—of women of course, because the Nazis would not allow any other public role for women—she found an outlet for her as yet unsatisfied ambitions. Even the Nazis' anti-bourgeois slogans and plebeian language had some appeal to her to whom bourgeois society and its morality had not been too kind. Recently she told me that she had turned her back on the Church long before this became fashionable for Nazi supporters.

In the end, Käte paid a price for her political folly when, after Hitler's downfall, she found herself in prison, or rather a detention camp. I understand that, in the trial she had to undergo, nobody accused her of any wrongdoing towards an individual, or of having obtained personal advantages. After more than a year she was released. Her husband died while she was detained. One of her sons was killed in the war, another lost an eye, and the third also suffered some damage to his health in the army and, as a prisoner of war, in France. In 1945, for the second time, the foundations of her existence were shaken; at her age a new start was not easy. However, without complaining, she kept herself alive by working for farmers in the fields, often sharing her food with others, until she was awarded her small widow's pension.

Among my relatives there were some, both older and younger, who steadfastly refused to conform, accepting the risks involved. As often happened in those years, the rift between pro-Nazis and others in the family was deep; communication virtually ceased until after 1945. As for myself, it took me several years after the end of the war before I felt able to resume any relations with former Nazis in the family.

Was I in any way affected by anti-semitism and aware of its existence as I grew up? The subject was rarely mentioned in my childhood days. Pogroms against Jews, such as occurred during that period in Eastern Europe, especially Russia and Poland, did not take place in Germany. Yet there was discrimination. I knew, for example, that before 1918 Jews (unless baptised) could not be university professors. There were no laws against Jews becoming army officers or government officials, but in fact they rarely obtained such posts. Only in exceptional cases did government officials have social relations with Jews, even though the Kaiser had Jewish friends. As far as I remember, my parents avoided inviting Jews to any of the dinner parties they were obliged to give because of father's official position. On informal occasions it was different. A Jewish friend of my brother Walter, with whom he was doing the one-year compulsory military service which the educated young men were allowed to do (three years otherwise), was a welcome guest. Still, even this was unusual. On an earlier occasion, one of mother's former school friends, a Jewess, visited us with her children. We children took this in our stride, but became rather perturbed when told that we were to return the visit. Talking among ourselves we wondered whether it would be safe to eat food in a Jewish home. It appears, therefore, that we were not unaffected by anti-semitic propaganda, even though it did not emanate from our home. Since the food tasted exceptionally good, we were cured of this prejudice, wherever it came from.

Few Jewish children were with me in the schools I attended up to the age of fifteen, but there were many at the grammar school, which was situated in a district of Berlin where many Jewish families lived. Among my fellow students of medicine, too, there were many Jews. Thus over the years I became accustomed to visiting Jewish homes. However, the racial origin of my friends scarcely interested me; few of them were orthodox believers.

Soon after the war, I joined a discussion group on topical political questions and their historical background. Everyone was given a subject on which to prepare a paper. The subject assigned to me was anti-semitism in Germany. So I had to study the phenomenon, and was shocked by what I discovered. I realised, however, that a relatively small section of the population was affected by this poison. Only sixteen Members of the Reichstag, for example, formed an anti-semitic group at that time. Because German Jews had long been trying to become assimilated as much as possible, the facts about anti-semitism were not greatly publicised. Nobody would have believed that persecution of the Jews such as occurred only two decades later could ever be possible.

The question of racial origin assumed importance for most people only when the Nazis started digging up records of people's ancestors, or inventing them when it suited their purpose. How ignorant people were about race, the "Aryan" race in particular, was reflected in the following joke circulating in the early days of Hitler. A citizen with little formal education, anxious to prove his Aryan origin to escape persecution, wrote to the clergyman of his native village: "Please send me my Arabian grandmother; she lies buried in your churchyard".

Only after the Nazis had seized power did I, for example, learn about one of my husband's grandfathers having been Jewish. My husband himself had not known this; his mother and other relatives had thought it wise to keep him in ignorance on this matter. His grandfather, so I was told later, had become a Christian in order to improve the marriage prospects of his four daughters. He had been successful in the case of my mother-in-law who had been able to marry an army medical officer. This instance throws some light on the climate of opinion which prevailed in Germany at the end of the nineteenth and in the first decades of the twentieth century.

There was sufficient evidence, before 1933, of a background of anti-semitic tendencies and certainly of Hitler's intentions against the Jews. His early programmatic book, *Mein Kampf,* was outspoken on the subject. Yet many Jews refused to believe that these diatribes would ever be turned into action; many, Jews and others, refused to read the book, which was indeed sickening. After 1933, when the floods of anti-semitic propaganda and terror were let loose, many Jews I knew still delayed leaving Germany until it was too late, and perished in the gas chambers of Hitler's extermination camps. They indulged in wishful thinking because they were proud of the contributions Jews had made to German economic and cultural life, and of their loyal service in the German army. Germany was home for them, and, like most other people, they were not attracted by the prospect of having to start from scratch elsewhere.

II

Revolt Against Tradition

How did it happen that I revolted against the ideas of my conservative, Protestant, middle-class environment?

From father's diary it appears that I was an amiable, cheerful child, easy to manage, often entertaining the whole family. Only one entry points in a different direction. Father wrote: "At times, however, she has very much a will of her own". At school, I got on well without too much of an effort. There was time for me to play, to read, to dream. For I was a dreamer as well as an avid reader. Often I was teased about my absentmindedness. Once mother gave me special praise because I had found in a trice the laundry cupboard from which she had asked me to fetch something. At Wiesbaden, where I spent the years between the ages of five and ten, I had to walk a long distance to school; only on rare occasions were we given money for the tram. I kept myself going by populating the lamp posts on the road with figures of my imagination, and each day I so to speak called on them for a chat, or on others who had replaced them at my whim. Later, in the Berlin suburb of Lichterfelde, it seems that I behaved in a similar way. Often on my way home from school my sister Hilde would walk closely in front of or behind me, but I would not notice her until we both landed at our front door.

The idea that I would go on to university arose early in my mind. It had its origin in a dream, the dream of going to India as a doctor to help the women forbidden by custom to be examined by a male doctor, and often left without medical attention. One of mother's cousins, on leave in Germany from her missionary work in India, visited our home at Wiesbaden, and impressed me deeply with her tales. She must have sensed the eagerness with which I, then a child of nine, responded. For she took me into the garden where we walked round the lawn, talking, talking. "It is no good," she assured me, "to administer to the spirit when the body is uncared for. I wished I had become a doctor as well as a missionary." This sounded convincing to me. Then she asked me: "Will you become a doctor

16

and go out to India?" I said, yes, I would. I told nobody about this, but for many years I continued to dream about my future life in India.

When I became aware of the fact that dreams, any dreams, required action for their realisation I began to think about the steps I would have to take for a professional career. In my type of family it was taken for granted that sons would study. That daughters might do the same was a relatively new thought, which in our home, at any rate, was not encouraged. I, the fifth daughter, was the first to go to university, and I remained the only one. Kurt and Walter had an academic education as of right; Ernst-Richard would have followed suit had he not done so badly at school. However, when my parents saw that I was determined, they raised no objections. With a certain resignation, father wrote: "In the winter of 1912/13 M. discovered in herself a liking for learned studies and began to learn Latin". In fact, when I told my parents about these Latin lessons, I had been taking them for a considerable time, earning the necessary money by helping younger pupils with their home work. I had not asked my parents for this money as I thought they could ill afford it. Moreover, I considered it good strategy to face them with some accomplished facts. I was by then used, in any case, to providing out of my own earnings for extras such as theatre tickets, skating or small gifts.

"Learned studies" did not describe exactly what I was after. I had missed a few years of grammar school, and without Latin I could not obtain admission to a form corresponding to my age. My intention was still to study medicine, even though the Indian dream was gradually fading into the background. As an alternative I considered for a time a career in publishing because of contact with a relative who belonged to the well-known Kiepenheuer publishing house, and because books meant much to me. However, I was looking for an alternative, mainly because of my fear that the study of medicine would be too costly and take too long. No hope of a scholarship in those days.

This fear subsided when an uncle offered to pay for my fees at university, which, in the case of medicine, were rather high. When he learned that I had become engaged to be married, he wanted me to promise that I would delay marriage until the end of my studies. I understood his practical considerations, but how could I give a promise for several years which I might not be able to keep? My own future then seemed as uncertain as that of the Weimar Republic in Germany. My refusal to give such a promise disappointed my uncle. Surprisingly, father came to my rescue. He, too, asked for a promise, but it was one I could honestly give: until my first medical examination, which was less than a year ahead, I was to refrain from active political work. I had neglected my studies because, as I shall describe in Chapter IV, I had become involved in the political events of 1918–1919, to my parents' obvious distress. Thus I needed to concentrate on my medical studies, in any case, if I was to pass the examination. Father may well have hoped that a year's pause would be sufficient to keep me from "becoming another Rosa Luxemburg", as he put it. He probably thought that this youthful aberration could not last. However, I recall gratefully that he did not ask for more, and I quite enjoyed the brief respite from politics. After a year's hard study, I had no difficulty in passing the examination with good marks. It almost did not take place because of a general transport strike in Berlin which made it difficult for professors as well as students to appear at the appointed places. Somehow, nearly all managed it.

Earlier on mother, too, had asked me for a promise. She was worried that I might get married without the domestic skills she considered vital and which indeed I lacked. I had not lived up to my parents' hope when they gave me the names Maria and Martha—the hope that I would be as pious a disciple of Jesus as Maria and as good a housewife as Martha. While I felt unable to give mother any reassurance on religious devotion, I tried to put her mind at rest on the question of domesticity. I promised that in the next long vacation I would devote time to learning the essentials of housekeeping. Nothing came of this in the end, as I became ill. However, I managed my domestic affairs more or less satisfactorily. In later years I even became good at cooking, and enjoyed it.

Although my pursuit of "learned studies" was not in line with my parents' views on a daughter's education, it proved easy to obtain their agreement. After all, I was not one of the pioneers; the way towards equal opportunities in education had been smoothed by others, some of whom I was fortunate enough to meet later, remarkable women like Minna Cauer and Helene Stöcker. Moreover, at least during certain periods, my four older sisters had not been content with being house-daughters waiting for a marriage partner. Grete had trained as a nurse, and Käte—under the pressure of circumstances, it is true—became a child care worker. Lucie and Hilde volunteered for nursing during the war, and my parents were proud of their response to a call of patriotism, although they missed the house-daughters and were happy when Lucie returned home because her fiancé was opposed to her nursing other men (he had been her patient!). I thought this a disgusting and typically male attitude. How could my sister stand for it, I wondered. But Lucie was so gentle and selfless that one could not be cross with her.

My struggle to break with the Church caused more difficulties than my diversion from traditional paths in education. It was not easy to clarify the issues for myself. Moreover, I could not avoid hurting my parents if I was to be honest. I loved and respected them and felt that I could not be dishonest towards them. Perhaps, I thought, they might understand if not approve, but this hope was in vain. They were probably too deeply hurt. How else could I explain mother's last words to me on her death bed when she pleaded with me to promise that I would return to the Church? I had to turn away, unable to give her this solace. This agonising experience made me even more critical of a doctrine which caused people to be so dogmatic and unfair. My bitterness was increased by the tactless sermon at mother's funeral by Kurt, my eldest brother. In front of the large gathering, he referred to the sorrow I had caused mother by forsaking the true faith, a sorrow which, he said, equalled that resulting from Grete allowing her children to be brought up as Catholics. Perhaps, like mother when she was dying, he was naive enough to believe that I could be induced by his words at her graveside to change my views.

There were five clergymen (including a female one) in the three generations of my family known to me, but they included none of mother's four brothers, who actually tended to be less orthodox than their sisters. One confessed to me once that he was unable to believe in the rigid way mother did. Yet to none of my relatives would the thought have occurred that anyone belonging to their family would openly oppose, or even leave, the Church. It would have been considered a social disgrace, let alone the religious aspects of the matter. Later I wondered whether these were perhaps the reasons why I was not invited to the weddings of my sisters Elisabeth and Inge. At the time, I hardly noticed it, for I had little contact with them, and was engrossed in the entirely different kind of life on which I had embarked.

Father was, on the whole, inclined towards a more liberal attitude than mother. He had a sense of humour which discouraged rigidity. I remember the delightful story he used to tell about his lessons prior to his confirmation. Girls and boys attended them together, but a curtain divided the sexes. The parson would stand in front where he could see all the children, who had great fun piercing holes through the curtain and throwing bits of paper with messages to each other. Mother greatly disliked this story, but father enjoyed telling it and teasing her a little.

It is possible that father was influenced by his early connections with the French Reformed Church to which his parents belonged. They were descendants of French Huguenots, so we were told, and our name Saran was an indication. As far as I remember, hardly any emphasis was placed on the French part of our heritage, perhaps because documentary proof of our ancestors' origin in France was not available. Once, during a holiday visit to East Prussia as a young girl, I visited my grandmother's grave at Königsberg, and I was surprised to find that the inscription on her grave stone was in French. In grandmother's time French had evidently still been in use at services of that Church. There is proof of French Huguenots among mother's ancestors, in the Bremen branch. I found it interesting to learn recently that at least one political revolutionary was among my maternal ancestors, too. It intrigued me to read a very interesting document, a long letter from a cousin of grandfather Florens Kriege, describing the revolutionary events in Berlin in 1848 in which he took an active part on the liberal anti-monarchist side. He was in Berlin on a visit from the USA whither he had emigrated. The prospects of Germany's political future seemed to him very gloomy; he foresaw long periods of reactionary rule. He tried to persuade his apparently conservative parents to go with him on his return to the USA and settle there. In my youth I certainly never heard about all this.

Notwithstanding his more relaxed attitude, father leaned strongly on the Church, which was a central pillar of his life. He was a leading member of the local "Bible club" which met alternately in different homes to study and discuss texts from the Bible. He was as upset as mother would have been, had she still been alive, about my decision to marry without the blessings of the Church. "But, surely, you cannot just live together like animals or heathen," he exclaimed. Then, less excitedly, he added: "Talk it over with our parson". I had done that already, and found him understanding. He was a progressively-minded man and, having followed my development over the years, he was not surprised about my decision. He remembered that I had come to him seven years before, a few days before my confirmation, to tell him of my religious doubts. I had been worried about the pledge I was to give to the Church, of whose teachings I had become critical. On that occasion he had persuaded me to go ahead by assuring me that I had to promise no more than that I would try. I was too young, he had said, for a final decision on these matters. The wording of the pledge, I had replied, seemed rather definitive to me; the formula used at the ceremony, which I succeeded in tracing, bears me out. It ran like this:

Minister: If you will to walk in that faith, to abjure sin and to follow your Saviour, then bear witness to this by acknowledging your baptismal vows.

Candidates: We renounce the Devil and all his works and ways, and commit ourselves to Thee, O Triune God, Father, Son and Holy Ghost, to serve Thee in loyal faith and obedience until our lives' end. Amen.

Minister: Will you also, so that you may have the strength to do all this, use in good conscience the means of grace provided for you? Will you be diligent in prayer, faithful to God's word and in attendance at his Table? Will you submit yourselves readily to the order and discipline of the Church? And will you by God's help continue as loyal members of our gospel church, sound in faith and godly in life, until the end? Then answer Yes we will, God being our helper.

Candidates: Yes we will, God being our helper.

Reluctantly, I had then accepted the parson's interpretation, relieved to see a way of avoiding the upheaval at home which would have resulted from my refusal to be confirmed. It would have meant no festivity, no guests, no gifts. Naturally, I was not indifferent to these aspects of the matter.

Käte, to my surprise, told me recently that I had confided my doubts about being confirmed and cried on her shoulder. I told nobody else at home about them, and she did not know what to suggest. In conflicts of any kind I got used to expecting no help from my family, and, as a result, withdrew more and more. Thus I acquired a certain reserve which I found difficult to shake off later. I only succeeded in doing so when I became much older.

It was several years later, in 1919, a few days before my marriage when I once again saw the parson who had confirmed me in spite of my doubts. This time the parson made no attempt to persuade me to have a church service after the registration of the marriage. My wedding day on 24 December 1919 thus passed without a religious rite. Indeed it lacked any kind of ceremony. It was Christmas Eve, and I had to do some shopping before going to the registry office, since the shops closed early. I remember that tiny room where I had difficulty in finding somewhere to place a large loaf of bread and other purchases. We had hardly had time to find the two witnesses, having decided rather hurriedly on the date because my husband's mother had died and he was left alone in their flat. We went home—without the witnesses—for lunch with father and, I believe, one or two sisters present. The topic of the marriage was not mentioned. It was a dismal kind of goodbye to my parental home.

There is no particular incident or outside influence to which I could trace my break with the Church. I cannot explain why only I among ten children subjected to the same conditions should have become a disbeliever in my youth. I simply had a deep longing for a rational, undogmatic, intellectually and morally satisfying philosophy of life, a longing which had grown gradually. My sisters often tried to persuade me not to show my doubts and disagreements. "Think what you like," they would say, "but keep quiet and conform for the sake of harmony and peace." On

many a Sunday morning they would say this when I had remained silent
after mother's usual question at breakfast: "Who goes to church with us?"
My refusal to go did not make for a happy Sunday atmosphere.

On some Sundays my parents would hold a service in our drawing
room, when because of illness or some other reason they could not go to
church. However, the rule of church service on Sundays was not too
rigidly followed. On some Sundays the parents missed it altogether and
took their children to the woods instead, and in this even the youngest
would take part.

Soon after I had been confirmed in 1912, I tried to avoid attending
church services whenever I found it possible. But when the First World
War started, I became for once a keen church goer. At that time I began to
reflect more deeply not only about religious and doctrinal problems but
about the political function of the Church. I saw it acting as an instrument
of the state, a reactionary German state at war, rather than a religious
institution practising the love of neighbour which it preached. The mixture
of Christianity and belligerent patriotism nauseated me. I was also appalled
by the thought that in "enemy" countries, too, God was called upon to
help on their side.

So why did I go to church more frequently then? I wanted to discover
whether all who preached the gospel spoke in the same vein. Thus for a
time I went to a different church in Berlin every Sunday. I found one
remarkable exception in the west end of Berlin in the Reverend Lesseur (I
believe this is how he spelled his name). His courage in refusing to defend
the war impressed me. These exploratory excursions were not to my
parents' liking, who rightly saw in them as much an indication of my
critical attitude as in my staying away from church service altogether.
Moreover, Lesseur had the reputation of being a socialist as well as a critic
of the war.

If the ideas of this parson were in fact socialist-inspired, this was all the
more reason for me to respond positively. The experience of the war and
of the rôle of the Churches in the war were intensifying my previous
misgivings about the social and political system on which German
imperialism and its drive towards war rested. I would not have called
myself a socialist then, nor had I any knowledge of or contact with the
socialist movement. But I was developing in that direction.

Feelings against social injustice caused by the system of society rather
than by evil intentions or deeds of individuals began to stir in me even in
my childhood days. Some instances stand out clearly in my mind.

At the age of eight or nine I began to learn French at school. Chatting
with our maid, who helped with putting the younger children to bed, I

discovered that she had never had such a chance simply because her parents were poor, and the ordinary schools which poor children attended did not teach languages. "This is not right," I thought, and I offered to teach her French in the evenings, recapitulating what I had just learned myself. It was a poor effort, and it was short-lived, but it signified the beginning of an awareness of the class society in which I lived. I also remember wondering sometimes why in our house at Dahlem the maids' room, where they liked to sit, had no central heating, and why it was smaller and more poorly equipped than our rooms were.

One Christmas Eve, when I was eleven years old, mother asked me to acompany her on her traditional visit to the poor. There were not many to be found where we lived, but there were a few agricultural workers housed on an old state farm which was still kept going. For the first time I entered some of these miserable crowded cottages. I almost was sick. Why should anybody have to live under such horrible conditions, especially children? In addition, these people were supposed to be grateful for Christian charity. Instinctively I felt that the position was as humiliating for these poor families as it was for us who brought them gifts. None of my sisters remembers having the same impression on such visits.

In our sheltered garden suburb, at school with other children from comfortably placed families, we had only occasional glimpses into the realities of working-class life as it existed in other parts of Berlin. Such occasions were, for example, the visits we children paid to father's older half-sister, a widow who lived on a small pension in East Berlin. She occupied one room in a large block of one- and two-room flats; toilets off the staircase shared by many tenants; no bathroom facilities; no separate kitchens. Compared to much of what I used to see later, as a social worker, the accommodation was not too bad, but the contrast to our own environment was striking. This aunt was always welcome as a guest in our house, but after a while she would become restless and leave. It was clear that apart from her independence she valued the daily contacts with her neighbours. I had an inkling of the closer community, the natural and informal mutual help relations often found in working-class areas—and often lost when slums are cleared and people moved to more spacious, healthier housing estates.

Another early experience comes back to my mind in this context. One day, like a flash of lightning, I perceived an unusual scene of exploitation. This happened on a visit to the Zoological Gardens in Berlin. As a special attraction a village of African natives was on show. Whole families were housed there in open huts, cooking outside their dwellings, behaving as they would at home—or so we were told—home being somewhere in a German colony. There they were, fascinating dark-skinned people, shivering in clothes meant for a warmer climate, or naked in the case of the children, stared at by the milling crowds of visitors just like the animals next door. Surely, I thought, it was wrong to use people thus as objects of exhibition to entertain others. I felt ill at ease. Yet, a year or two later, taken along by a school friend, I danced happily through the night at a ball organized by the *Verein für das Deutschtum im Ausland,* one of the associations supporting Germany's "cultural mission" abroad among "primitive" races. Only when, under the impact of the war, I started critically to analyse social conditions, did I begin to understand colonialism as part of an evil system, as a reflection of low moral standards on the colonialists' side.

During the war years I became increasingly aware of the gulf which divided me from my parents in political as well as religious matters. I was not trying then to defend socialism as against conservatism. I had not yet any clear idea as to where my feelings for social justice would lead me. The controversial issue was the war, German politics regarding the war, to be more precise.

As far as I know, my parents, who were traditionally conservative with remnants of a feudal outlook, did not belong to a political party. After the war they probably voted for the German National Party, the party farthest to the right, since they did not welcome the birth of a democratic republican state. The Monarchy had always seemed to them the historically given and desirable system which provided stability and order in the German Empire. When father referred in his diary to his ambition of being transferred to Berlin to serve in the ministry, he wrote—the formulation was significant: "I want to be close to the centre of the Monarchy". Audiences with Emperor William II on architectural projects were among the highlights in his career, and were noted in his diary. We children would be excited to see him leave the house in his splendid civil servant's uniform and, on his return from the Palace, listen to his story, especially once when the Empress had been present, and father had graciously been allowed to pick up her ball of knitting wool.

Before 1914, politics had hardly been discussed at home; at least I have no memory of it. The First World War, not only in Germany, aroused people's sense of patriotism and brought political matters to the fore. Jingoism became widespread; "Germany, or the Kaiser, can do no wrong" was the motto also in our family. Both my feeling and my intelligence were offended by anything resembling "hurrah-patriotism", as it was called. Perhaps from the beginning I was less inclined towards any enthusiasm for the war than others because I happened to be on holiday in

East Prussia when the war broke out. Not far from the frontier, faced with an immediate threat of a Russian invasion, the people there reacted more soberly than the Berlin population. Many fled from the areas where Russian troops entered.

For my parents, with their strong sense of duty, patriotism carried an obligation to help; they took an East Prussian refugee family of five into our not exactly empty house until their return to the reconquered province was possible. A government commission was then sent there to plan for reconstruction, and father went with it as an adviser. I remember a photograph showing him standing by the side of Field Marshal Hindenburg, victor in the battle of Tannenberg, in which an estimated 130,000 Russian soldiers, encircled and driven into the Mazurian swamps, had perished or been taken prisoner. Their horrible fate aroused no pity on the German side as far as I could observe. In war, the enemy deserved no pity; this was the accepted doctrine everywhere. For the Russians in particular, there was no sympathy in Germany. Fear of the "barbarians" from the east had swayed even many in the labour movement to abandon their opposition to war. Ignoring German aggression and invasion of neutral countries in the west, and the fact that the German declaration of war against Russia had preceded that of Russia against Germany, if only by one day, many supported and justified the war as a defensive war.

Soon after my return to Berlin from the anxieties of the East Prussian situation, I had something like a traumatic experience. Many of the German troops were switched from the western front, where they had rapidly advanced, to the threatened east. My brother Walter (Kurt, being a clergyman, was exempted from military service) was among them. We had been notified of the time when his train would stop in Berlin. In the middle of the night, our whole family, including even the smaller children, went to the station to see him. The scene at that station, with hundreds of laughing, boisterous young soldiers, my brother touched to see us all, stands before me as if it was yesterday. There were the inscriptions chalked on the railway carriages: "Off to Paris", "Smash the enemy", "Total victory for Germany", "The Czar to the gallows", "Perfidious Albion". Soon after that night, Walter was reported "missing"; he never returned. We had all been fond of him. He had been a good friend to his younger sisters. He had carried our bags when he happened to meet us on our way home from school at Wiesbaden on hot, sticky days; he had spent many hours together with father making furniture for our dolls' house; he had relieved me of the fish I disliked and smuggled it on to his plate when mother was not looking.

Perhaps it was in that night at the station that the first serious doubts were born in my mind about the sense of it all. It was a great relief to me when, later, I found others who shared these doubts. These included Max Hodann, my future husband, whom I met in politically interested circles of the youth movement to which a school friend introduced me during my last year at grammar school. Then I discovered that the opposition to the proclaimed German war aims was growing in the country. Even after the military fortunes had begun to turn against the German side, the annexation of large territories was still among these aims. Those in opposition saw these claims as a barrier to a peace by negotiations and, prophetically, a sure acceleration of disaster for Germany.

In Germany there was much less opposition on general pacifist grounds than, I learned later, existed in Britain. Unlike the British, the German law did not allow any exemptions from military service on grounds of conscience—as it does now in post-war Germany. Nevertheless, there were war resisters, some of them altogether critical of the régime of the Kaiser and what it stood for; they went to prison rather than become soldiers. But the opposition which developed during the war centred on German politics which, it was felt, were responsible for prolonging the fighting. "Peace without annexations" was what they proclaimed.

One of my uncles, the eldest of mother's brothers, who held a prominent position in the Foreign Office, had strong reservations on some of Germany's policies. He was opposed to annexationist demands. I believe he often supported the views of the Chancellor, Bethmann-Hollweg, as against those of the military or the Kaiser. Sometimes he voiced his critical opinions openly in the family circle. I remember in particular his comments on the decision in 1917 to start an all-out U-boat war. "This is disastrous," Uncle Johannes Kriege said sternly and sadly, "for it will bring the United States of America into the war, and eventually mean our total defeat". It became clear before long how right he was. Mother kept quiet because she respected her brother. At home, however, she would not allow critical comments on the Kaiser or the army or the U-boat war or any other official policy.

Once a cousin, on home leave from the front, visited us. He talked about his own experiences, the cruelties he had seen committed by Germans, the mistakes for which, in his opinion, German army leaders were responsible. Mother virtually shut him up. She did not want to hear any more; it simply could not be true. I did not like this cousin, but on that day I sympathised with him. Soon after this visit, he was killed in battle.

Meals in those years were ordeals for me. Invariably the war news was discussed, as presented by the right-wing, pro-war papers which came into our home. I sat through these meals in silence, for I felt it was hopeless to question or argue. I found a certain consolation in the thought that it might be good for me to practise self-restraint and self-discipline. As I disliked the nationalist tone of the papers read at home, I ordered a liberal newspaper for myself; I believe it was the *Berliner Tageblatt*. This was not an anti-war or anti-establishment paper by any means, but its appearance in our home caused an uproar.

The tensions over politics seemed to me worse than the food shortages, although these were not negligible. We were able to supplement our rations a little by produce from the garden, and we gave some to others. Mother refused on principle to buy anything on the black market. Often she denied herself some of her own rations so as to give more to the children. We of the younger generation were less strict in this respect, or perhaps just less prepared to go hungry. Lucie's fiancé, like others who served behind the front in the agricultural areas in the east occupied by Germany, sometimes sent us food parcels. We did not inquire into the legality, or morality, of our getting these parcels from "enemy" territory. Usually, to avoid argument, we consumed the delicious extra provisions when our parents were out.

I tried to define my attitude to patriotism, but I was reluctant to disown it altogether, as were many others who were no "hurrah-patriots" either. Significantly, one radical group which opposed the German war aims called itself "New Fatherland". Fatherland, yes, but a new kind! Yet even in the existing one with all its faults I could not help thinking about those suffering and dying at the front, most of whom had not joined the army of their own free will. Could one, so to speak, stab them in the back? Did we who were spared their fate not owe them some solidarity? These were vexing questions to which I could see no clear answers.

Before starting my first term of medical studies at Berlin University, I had two or three months to spare. I volunteered to help in a canteen at a Berlin railway station where soldiers were served meals and refreshments. I realised that this meant doing something for the war effort, yet it gave me some satisfaction to serve in this practical way. In this canteen I was nicknamed "the Botticelli girl". Apparently I did not look like a rebel but more like the Madonna on the pictures of this Italian painter.

It was during my last year at school that I began to break out of my intellectual isolation. The university offered further opportunities to find like-minded people. The group of the youth movement to which I was attracted tended to the left. It was called "German *Wandervogel*", *Wandervogel* meaning wandering bird, a term used for many sections of the youth movement. I do not remember why this group added the word

German to its name; it was not nationalistic, but keen on cultural and social issues besides the usual camping activities. Here I was, at a relatively late stage, learning to sleep in tents or haystacks, swim in cold lakes, march many miles with a heavy rucksack, sing around camp fires. It was good training in many respects. We learned to bear hardships, and to use our leisure time in a healthy community atmosphere.

Members of the youth movement were in revolt against traditional fashions and ways of life, in other words they abandoned hats, high-heeled shoes and stays, and refused alcohol and nicotine. When I first appeared in the loose smocks worn by reform-loving young men and women alike (how similar fashions are today) I was told off by my elders. They said I looked continually pregnant, but I did not care. I had my hair cut short at a time when it was still a rather daring thing to do.

More important than all this were for me the contacts with politically minded leaders whom I met in the youth movement. I was eager to learn from them. Many, like myself, later joined the political Labour movement. In those days I was shy, and just listened to what others were saying in discussions. I did not even dare to put questions in any larger gathering.

Towards the end of the war, a friend invited me to hear Ernst Toller read his first play. This poet and playwright became famous in the inter-war period; in 1919 he was Prime Minister in the short-lived Bavarian Soviet Republic and subsequently imprisoned for five years. The play was a passionate outcry against the war. In the drawing room of a flat in Berlin's West End we sat without a break, listening as if in a trance. When Toller had finished and put his manuscript on the table beside him, he sat still, looking pale, spent and exhausted. No one moved, no one said a word. The silence seemed to last an eternity; I felt that it could not go on. So I conquered my shyness and went to Toller to thank him. This broke the ban. That same night I also wrote to him, still under the strong impression of his anti-war play. In reply he sent me two or three poems he had scribbled down. I treasured them, but they were lost in the 1933 upheaval.

On the following Sunday, we walked together in Berlin's famous woods, the *Grunewald*. The next I heard was that Toller had been arrested. Before coming to Berlin, he had led a students' anti-war protest at Heidelberg University, and had been sent down by the authorities. His connections with munition workers on strike, a more dangerous thing to be involved in during the war than students' protests, led to his arrest in Berlin and his subsequent imprisonment until the 1918 Revolution opened the prison gates.

My letter to Toller was found among the papers in his room. So there was a sequel for me, too. Two secret police agents appeared at our house. Fortunately, Hilde, who was closest to me, was alone at home. She was just hanging up the laundry in the garden, where they found her. She seems to have dealt skilfully with the agents, even though she was shocked at first; they said they would refrain from any further steps, "in consideration of the respect in which your father is held", as they explained. We did not tell anybody about this visit, and it was not repeated.

Max Hodann, by that time no longer in Berlin, was also on the lists of politically suspect people because of his activities among students. Action had been taken against him, too. Instead of being allowed to finish his medical studies first—a concession often made because of the shortage of fully-trained doctors—he was called up and made an army doctor. He was sent to occupied Poland, to a remote spot, a camp for "delousing" troops in transit. Soon he discovered that he had a "nursemaid"; a man who was watching his every step was occupying a room next to his. Letters to me arrived irregularly, often in big bundles, whenever the censor decided to send them on. Mother could not understand why "our efficient field post" suddenly behaved so erratically. The idea that censorship was to blame was far from her mind. By that time, I had become so uncommunicative that she had only the vaguest notion of what I was thinking and doing.

Long after the war, when we were supposed to live under a civilian republican instead of a military monarchist régime, my husband found out by chance that the same lists were still in use—a confirmation of the lack of republican thoroughness in cleaning up the old civil service.

III

Marriage and Profession

On the whole my married life was not happy, and, after seven years, we obtained a divorce. Even before the divorce, we had lived separately for some years, but until my husband wished to marry again we continued to live in the same flat. We were good friends. Though we had agreed to go our own personal ways, we shared ideas and activities. Sometimes we found ourselves in slightly embarrassing situations. In 1924, for example, for different reasons both Max and I visited Britain. I attended an international trade union summer school at Ruskin College, Oxford, and then spent some time in London trying to get to know the Labour and socialist movement. Max was especially keen to visit the London museums but also took up contact with the Labour movement. With the help of the Independent Labour Party (ILP) I was put up by a working-class family at Kentish Town, and could not have had a better introduction to the London of the Cockneys, their humour and warm hospitality. To my surprise, Max, who had arrived a little later and had also contacted the ILP, was sent to the same family on the assumption that we would not mind sharing a bed.

It took me a long time to admit even to myself that I was unable to live with Max Hodann. It took so long because I hesitated to hurt him and he did not want to part from me. The agreement which existed between us on many things that mattered had seemed a good basis for an enduring partnership—many of our friends had also thought so. We were both freethinkers (later I preferred the term "agnostic"—or, more positive— humanist), although there was a certain difference in our approach because Max never had to struggle, as I had, to become free of church and family ties. His mother, who was widowed when he was very young, had lived solely for her son. She had spoilt him in a way that I often found intolerable, and I believe this explained in part a weakness in him which made him personally very dependent on others. His mother had never opposed anything he wanted to do, and from early on, followed his ideas and wishes rather than trying to insist on any of her own.

30

We were both keen internationalists, and, from early youth, socialist-inclined. Only after the war did we join a political party, first the Independent Social Democratic Party (USPD) which had broken away from the Social Democratic Party (SPD) during the war, then the SPD—in 1921 after the USPD became re-united with it having lost one wing to the Communist Party. Max was three years older than I and endowed with a quick mind and many talents. As a teenager he had close contact with the family of Karl Kautsky, the prominent Labour leader and Marxist theoretician; he went to school with one of Kautsky's sons. This had a considerable influence on him though he was no disciple of Kautsky. He was looking for a new radical challenge, for a leadership which might inspire the idealistic youth whose experience of the war had made them critical both of the war and of the Labour leaders, but who were not attracted by communist doctrines. His attention was drawn to Leonard Nelson, a young philosopher at Göttingen University, who based himself on Kant and Fries. In a lecture on the eve of the outbreak of war Nelson had proclaimed the need for an international league of states. Throughout the war, and even after, he was one of the main targets of attack from the nationalist side. Göttingen University was a hotbed of jingoism.

Max was impressed by Nelson's writings, by his ethical teachings and by his personality. In one of our first encounters he told me about Nelson, saying: "He is not well known, but I believe that he is one of the few personalities in our time who count". Before Max left for his military assignment at the delousing camp in Poland, he urged me to study for a term or two at Göttingen, and I was able to do so. At Göttingen I eagerly joined the circle around Nelson, and the discussions held at his attic flat. Beside my medical studies this absorbed most of my time, and my devotion and loyalty were increasingly engaged. The interest in Nelson's ideas which Max and I had in common, and our active participation in the organisation for political education (IJB—*Internationaler Jugendbund*—International League of Youth), officially launched by Nelson in 1918, greatly strengthened our marriage ties. In the end, Max broke with Nelson at the same time as we finally separated, but he had felt critical for some time of the rigidity and utopianism (as he saw it) of Nelson's approach. Later he was often close to the communists, but he stated towards the end of his life that he never was a member of the Communist Party, preferring to take his stand as an independent left-wing intellectual. His second wife was an active communist.

Why was it that, despite the community of outlook, ideas and aspirations which reinforced our marriage, it did not work out? From the beginning there was in me a deep emotional resistance to this union in which, as I sensed, I would never find real fulfilment in love. But I did not listen to the warning voice within me, or, at any rate, silenced it again and again. Reserved and shy as I was, I did not talk to anybody about this. My mother-in-law, who saw us together at close quarters in her home, where I was received with great generosity and kindness, seems always to have feared that I might leave Max. She was instinctively aware of anything that threatened her son. In her feverish fantasies during her last short illness these fears came out. If it had not been for her sudden death I might still have avoided a formal commitment. Yet I cannot be sure about this. Probably the desire to leave my parental home moved me as strongly as the arguments in favour of this marriage. Moreover, I was too young and inexperienced for an honest self-analysis. Nor was I as free from certain traditional preconceptions as I imagined I was. Like many of my contemporaries, I stood for a new sexual morality, and therefore accepted pre-marital sexual relations without qualms. But I could not help feeling that such relations carried an obligation to permanency and should eventually lead to marriage.

A few years later I once sought the advice of a friend, the psychiatrist Arthur Kronfeld (who emigrated to Russia after 1933 and, like others, was never heard of again). I attended regularly Kronfeld's fascinating seminars on hypnosis at the Institute of Sexology.* The Institute's director was Magnus Hirschfeld, a world authority on the subject that Max Hodann had previously worked on for a time as an assistant at the Institute. Kronfeld sympathised with my dilemma, but proceeded to stress my husband's good qualities, the interests he and I had in common, and how much he was attached to me—as if I did not know all this. He suggested that I should stay with Max and try to make the best of it. He was persuasive, and I made some attempts, but in the end I felt unable to continue.

Our daughter Renate—who in Britain became Rene just as I changed from Maria to Mary, for the sake of easier pronunciation in the land of our refuge—was born in Copenhagen in 1921. Danish friends had invited me to spend the summer in Copenhagen where I would enjoy more restful conditions and have better food than was as yet available in Germany. Since Max had not yet found a permanent job, this offer was welcome. I made use of my stay in Denmark to become proficient in the Danish language. With this foundation, I easily acquired a good knowledge of the other Scandinavian languages, and when the need arose, I was able to earn money by translating from these languages. After 1950, in my work for the Socialist International, I used this knowledge extensively.

* This was the pioneering German Institute for the scientific study of sexual behaviour.

Soon after my return to Berlin with the baby, our financial problems were solved. Max became chief medical officer first at Nowawes, a town near Berlin, then in one of the twenty districts of Berlin under the progressive public health system established in the Weimar Republic. As a sideline he pursued his interest in sexology, writing and lecturing on the subject. He was good at popularization, and was well liked among young people. His first book *Bub und Mädel* ("Boy and Girl"), which he dedicated to "my friends in the Labour Youth movement" was widely read and has an appeal even today. Another book, *Bringt uns wirklich der Klapperstorch* ("Are we really brought by the stork?") was dedicated to Renate. Max retained his position until 1933. Like many other left-wing intellectuals he was arrested by the Nazis on the night of the Reichstag fire in January 1933. No specific accusations were brought against him, or any of the others. He was released after a few months as a result of efforts made by his second wife through friends abroad. In the early days of Hitler, such efforts sometimes still had success. He took no chances, but immediately left Germany. After a period in Norway, just before the German invasion he went to Sweden, where he died in 1946.

Renate was a delicate child, having inherited her father's disposition to bronchial asthma. Her first attack was the worst; she was hardly one year old then, and for a year I spent most of the day and the night carrying her around for fear that she might choke with coughing. At the age of nine she got rid of her asthma, with only one relapse, much later, in Britain.

There was no question, then, of resuming my medical studies. I had continued them for a while after I got married but had given them up to earn some money. I found a job in the newly established German Association for the League of Nations, which worked to prepare the ground for Germany's admission to the League. First I worked in the education department under the well-known Swiss Quaker, Elisabeth Rotten; then in the archives. It was a useful experience for an internationalist like myself.

It would have been possible for me to go back to my study of medicine after Renate, at the age of two, had been accepted in the children's section of the residential college, the *Walkemühle,* founded by Nelson and his coworker, Minna Specht. Both Max and I favoured her going to the *Walkemühle* on educational as well as on health grounds; it seemed better for the child to live in the country and in a group of children. Moreover, it would free me for the work I wanted to do.

What was the work I wanted to do? By then I had come to realise that I had to choose between making politics or medicine my main concern; I could not do both. It was not an easy choice. The precarious state of affairs in which, so soon after the disaster of the First World War, Germany and the world found themselves, coupled with my conviction that politics would determine the course of events, led me to the conclusion that as far as possible I should give priority to political work.

It is true that a completed medical training might have been useful after my divorce when I had to look for a job. But after my emigration to Britain, where the German qualifications counted for nothing, I would have been in no better position. It would have been impossible for me to repeat the whole of my studies, which would have needed money and many years for doing so. In those years, political tasks again demanded attention. I felt that it was urgent to warn the world of the Nazi threat and to help the anti-Nazis left behind in Germany.

Political work, when I made my choice, meant voluntary, unpaid work. I was earning a little by teaching in adult education courses, and the Berlin Trade Union Centre offered me welcome opportunities in this field. I enjoyed teaching adults, and saw some political value in it, too. In the main, however, I depended financially on my husband. This posed no problems as long as there was complete understanding between us about the purposes which we were both anxious to serve. After the divorce, when I needed an economic basis for myself, I was lucky to find a satisfactory solution fairly soon, satisfactory in two respects: the work as a social worker in a factory was interesting, and it left me a fair amount of time and freedom for political activities. I even acquired superannuation rights, acknowledged and honoured after the Second World War; not that I had counted on that! I almost missed the deadline for submitting the necessary application.

Renate's relations with her father were not disturbed by the unpleasantness which went with divorce proceedings and the final estrangement between her parents. At the time of the divorce, she was away, but even later, when she joined me again in Berlin in the flat I was then sharing with socialist friends, she was never adversely affected either. Later, she assured me emphatically that she could not remember any unhappiness in her childhood, and had missed nothing.

Max Hodann's second marriage was not a success for long. His kindness and weakness were exploited in an often unscrupulous manner. His second daughter had the same hysterical disposition as her mother, as was noticed by Renate on her visits to her father. All the same she spent enjoyable Sundays there. In the late thirties, after the final breakup of his second marriage, Max visited Britain and we met on amicable terms. He always took a warm interest in Renate to whom he often wrote and sent some of the lovely sketches he drew. I met him briefly by chance for the last time

in Paris, on his return from the Civil War in Spain where he had joined the
Republican army as a doctor. As a result of the hardships he had suffered
in Spain, his asthma returned, which caused his death at a rather early age.
With his third wife, with whom he had a son, he had found real happiness
in Sweden, where he worked at the Stockholm Institute of Sexology.
After the Second World War both Renate and I developed good relations
with her Swedish half-brother, Jan, and his mother. Later Jan's Swedish
wife and their children were happily included in this friendship.

The experience of fulfilment in love has not been denied me, and
personal ties have enriched my life. At times, I have known loneliness and
the pangs of separation when an intimate relationship came to an end.
Jealousy, too, has caused me some suffering. I have always fought it, most
of the time successfully, I believe. These were lonely battles since I was
reluctant to show or even admit to myself feelings of which I was
ashamed. I never considered marrying again. I have refrained in these
memoirs from any account in detail of experiences in personal relation-
ships. This does not mean that these were unimportant to me or that they
might be of no interest to others. It simply reflects a personal reserve
which is part of my nature, even though in the course of time I became so
much more outgoing than I had been in my younger days. More
important, it reflects the fact—which some might find strange—that the
main concerns and decisions in the life I had chosen were not determined
by these experiences. I find it deeply satisfying that memories of them
never held any bitterness, and that valuable friendships endured.

In my relations with Renate there were periods of tension and even
estrangement while she was in her teens and early twenties, although I
remember no real conflicts. Our relations have become increasingly close
and harmonious. It has been one of the blessings of my old age to share a
home with her and her husband.

IV

Entry into Politics

In 1918, when the First World War ended, I was only 21. But I cannot remember feeling really young, then or in the fifteen years that followed. My unhappy experience in married life was one reason. But more important was the pressure of political developments in Germany and the responsibility which I, like others, felt for their outcome. The weight of this pressure was hardly ever lifted. Perhaps this is why my hair turned white soon after I had reached the age of thirty. Sometimes during the war I had looked forward to dancing again when there was peace. But when peace came at last, we felt that all that must wait "till we have won the revolution". By "we" I mean the politically engaged young people, of whom I was one, who during the war had started working with Leonard Nelson and his circle at Göttingen. A social revolution was necessary if the return to nationalism and reaction in Germany was to be prevented—of this we were convinced. But we soon realized that the foundations laid in the Weimar Republic did not hold out much promise in that respect. Impressed by the rigorous ethical ideas embedded in Nelson's philosophy, we accepted for our own lives the consequences resulting from this situation. Whatever the weaknesses of the Weimar Republic, the struggle for justice had to be waged, and this had implications for one's personal life.

However serious we were, we were nevertheless glad to escape from the austerity of the war years. One day, a friend said to me—this was some time after rationing had been abolished: "Why don't you get a new dress—you are young after all". I was still wearing the clothes my mother-in-law had made for me during the war out of old curtain material and bed linen left from her dowry. My friend took me to a department store and persuaded me to buy three summer dresses. Three in one go—an extravagance I had never known before. To this day, because of the strong impression this purchase made on me, I remember exactly colour, fabric and pattern of these dresses. All were made of cotton and fairly long. One was in green and white stripes, another in big pale violet and white squares and the third was in small multi-coloured squares. The style was simple. However, the idea of dancing did not materialise until many years later, in Britain, when for the sake of sociability I joined in some dancing at Labour Party conference social events.

The collapse of the German army in 1918 and the overthrow of the Hohenzollern Monarchy found me at Göttingen in my fourth term of medical studies. So, in the days of the political upheaval in Berlin, I was far from the centre of the 1918/19 revolution. Max Hodann—this was typical of the time and the man—was anxious not to miss the epoch-making events in the capital. Instead of awaiting his orders in Poland, he made his way back to Berlin on his own, first cutting off the epaulettes and stripes from his (medical) officer's uniform so as to avoid being molested, and then making some propaganda for the Republic on the way. However, even in our small provincial town the revolution did not pass us by completely.

Among the students at Göttingen University at that time there were only a handful of socialists, most of them girls. We knew each other from the discussions held in Nelson's study on Nikolausberger Weg, because he had not yet started again to lecture or hold seminars at the university after a period of army service. This small group used to meet on most days at the city restaurant where cheap lunches were available, usually consisting of cabbage or turnips, sometimes with a few potatoes thrown in. There we sat together, talking about current events. Our excitement at the news about the November revolution was tremendous. We saw the dawn of a better era and were filled with great hopes. I remember only one other historic occasion when I felt equally elated: in London in May 1945, when the Second World War had ended and the nightmare of the Hitler régime was over.

A workers' and soldiers' council was spontaneously set up at Göttingen, as in other places throughout Germany. I felt I could not go on attending anatomy lectures or sit with my books in my icy room, as if nothing had changed. I therefore went to the new council to offer my services. It had installed itself in a small room, in the town hall I believe. The only male student in our circle, who belonged to a branch of the Labour movement, was included in the workers' and soldiers' council. When I appeared on the scene he had just gone to free the political prisoners, having obtained the prison keys without difficulty. I am afraid a few ordinary criminals also benefited by this liberating act.

The duties assigned to me were of a humbler nature. First of all I made a rubber stamp inscribed "Workers' and Soldiers' Council, Göttingen" from a box I had bought with my own money from a toy shop. This was needed for providing the soldiers returning from the army, which was in the process of dissolution, with a stamp on their papers which would enable them to obtain food ration cards. In the absence of any other authority we just took over and did what seemed necessary. Little did we worry at that moment whether there would be enough food to honour the rations. Hundreds of exhausted and disillusioned soldiers, whose one thought was to go home to the villages around Göttingen, passed the trestle tables behind which I was performing my revolutionary function.

Meanwhile the academic community had been stirred into action, too. A mass meeting at the university was convened to discuss the situation. Different viewpoints were expressed. Nobody dared openly to oppose the Republic; most just "took their stand on the basis of the facts", as the German saying goes (*sich auf den Boden der Tatsachen stellen*). We, the small band of socialists, sat in one of the front rows of the overcrowded hall. Should not one of us speak up for the Republic when the other speakers were at best lukewarm? The politically most knowledgeable among us was the one who had opened the prison doors, but he suffered from a bad stutter. Suddenly, they all whispered to me: "You must do it, you will know what to say". My name was sent up to the platform. So I had to speak, for the first time in public. In the circumstances, I acquitted myself not too badly. At once I learned what it means to expose yourself to the public eye. A student, member of a Catholic group, got up to denounce me for my lack of patriotism. She had overheard, so she said, a remark I had made in the city restaurant to the effect that one should send one's money out to Switzerland. I asked for the floor on a point of order, and repudiated the fantastic denunciation. This was my first taste of the rough and tumble of politics.

Soon everyday life returned to normal; law and order were restored. I went back to the Institute of Anatomy where I had a hostile reception since my political activities had become known among my fellow students, most of them right-wing in their inclinations. To reach the lecture hall, one had to climb two or three flights of stairs, laid out in stone. I was wearing wooden sandals at the time, which few people did, but in my large family we had run out of leather shoes. The sandals made a terrific noise on the stone stairs so that my arrival was announced long before I entered the hall. I was promptly received by the students making a noise with their feet, the usual way for German students to show disapproval. After a while they got tired of it. We were back to normal.

My first experience of public speaking had not filled me with an ardent desire for more. I wondered whether my political role could rather be that of a teacher, lecturer, discussion leader, perhaps writer. I was also prepared to take my share of organizational work, which I knew was always necessary. My inhibitions against public speaking were gradually overcome, but I always preferred activities in which reasoned arguments, a give and take of ideas, had a better chance to prevail than in platform speaking for propaganda purposes.

Rather unexpectedly I was launched as a speaker in one of the election campaigns in the early twenties. Mathilde Wurm, a Social Democratic Member of Parliament, who was always on the look-out for young women who could be encouraged to do political work, asked me whether I would address a few women's meetings in her constituency, Thuringia in Central Germany. I had met her at some gatherings where plans for community kitchens in blocks of flats were discussed. (Mathilde Wurm committed suicide after her escape to London in the early days of Hitler, probably out of despair, together with her young friend, Dora Fabian, also a friend of mine.) Women's meetings sounded like my cup of tea; I was confident that I could deal with the subjects required.

When I called at the headquarters of the SPD of Thuringia in Weimar I was informed that they had abandoned special women's meetings. I was handed my itinerary—all public meetings—and a copy of "Speakers' Notes" issued for the campaign. My timid protests were brushed aside. This was not a time for arguing. "You have a three- or four-hour journey before your first meeting", I was told, "plenty of time to prepare yourself".

The "Speakers' Notes" proved to be informative and helpful. I hardly ever studied anything as eagerly as this document. Someone who had watched me in the train told me later that he had wondered what I was up to! I wondered a little myself. Another surprise awaited me at my first place of destination. Not only was there to be no meeting for women, there was to be no SPD meeting on that day at all. The SPD had cancelled its own meeting because the German National Party was holding one with a well-known speaker who was expected to draw a crowd. It had been arranged that I would speak for the SPD in the discussion at that meeting. I put aside the notes I had jotted down in the train, and resigned myself to yet another role.

As I listened to the main speaker, I looked at the hard faces of the men on the platform, a dozen or so, most of them with scars from the sabre fighting customary in the reactionary German students' associations (*schlagende Verbindungen*). I felt a cold fury rising in me and indignation overcame my shyness when it was my turn to speak. I noticed at once that my words went home. I remember how I attacked these men and their party as being responsible for the murder of Walther Rathenau (24 June 1922), one of the ablest ministers in the early days of the Weimar Republic who had worked hard to restore economic stability and obtain less harsh terms for the reparations Germany had to pay to the Allies. I also denounced their talk of Christianity as sheer hypocrisy, and told them that, having been brought up as a Christian, I knew what I was talking about. All this, and more, from a fair young lady caused rather a sensation, and there was a tremendous applause from the workers who sat in the gallery.

At another election meeting in Thuringia I heard for the first time a speaker from the newly-born Nazi Party, which did not then organize meetings of its own, but sent its speakers to those of other parties. This man made such a poor impression that I would hardly have given his party a chance of success. How wrong I was! The Nazi's turn came last on that night; he started long after midnight. It was not customary to limit speaking time, so he went on for an hour, as the previous speakers had done. Yet people stayed to the end.

Among my early experiences of public meetings which I remember is that of a full-blown communist onslaught on a social democratic meeting, also in Thuringia—the first such attack I can recall, but it was by no means the last I witnessed. Even at that early stage in post-war developments, it was clear that extremism on the right represented a growing threat to the Republic and the entire Labour movement. The victory of Mussolini and the suppression in Italy of socialists and communists alike was the writing on the wall. Yet the thesis which inspired communist strategy and according to which social democrats were enemy number one, was followed to the bitter end. Eventually, social democrats and communists found themselves together in Hitler's prisons and concentration camps, some continuing their old disputes even there, others seeking to overcome them.

Thuringia, like Saxony, was a communist stronghold. It was there that the Communist Party had staged its ill-fated "Central German rising" in 1921, for which the workers had to pay and which resulted in a strengthening of reactionary forces. In October 1923 there was unrest again, after three communist ministers had been included in the Thuringian government, and the *Reichswehr* under Seeckt had intervened to remove them.

These events explain the background to the communist attack at the above-mentioned meeting. I vividly remember it: a small industrial town, a working class audience consisting in about equal numbers of social democratic and communist supporters, the uniformed *Reichsbanner* men (the *Reichsbanner* was an association of volunteers for the defence of the Republic) standing lined up in front of the platform to protect chairman and speakers. The atmosphere was tense from the start. After a few words from the first speaker, a local man, the expected uproar started. The communists shouted him down, ignored the chairman who kept ringing the bell to no avail, jumped on to chairs and tables and held up their beer glasses (beer was nearly always served at political meetings) ready to throw them at a given moment. Evidently, the communists had decided that the meeting was not to be allowed to proceed. In a moment of sudden inspiration I asked the chairman whether I might try to speak. He agreed, and I took the bell from him. When I rang it, everybody was so surprised that the noise stopped. I appealed to the audience to sit down as I wanted to say something before catching my train back to Berlin. They sat down, and without interruption listened to my speech which I wisely kept short. The local speaker, who followed me, was also heard; he too made a short speech. Somewhat prematurely, but in good order the meeting was closed. The *Reichsbanner* men followed behind me when I left the hall; nobody attacked us.

On that night, in that small town, even though bitterness was great because the army of the Weimar Republic, with the support of the SPD, had put down a workers' rising, common sense prevailed. The workers at least refrained from fighting each other. Alas, this case remained an exception. All attempts to form a common workers' front against the Nazi threat were condemned to failure.

V

Leonard Nelson, IJB and ISK

It was in December 1917 that I met Leonard Nelson for the first time. I
went to see him to ask whether, on my going to Göttingen for my next
term in the spring, I could participate in the philosophical discussions
which were being held in his study. I visited him in Berlin during the
seasonal holiday, when he was visiting his parents who lived in the
middle-class suburb of Westend.

At twenty, I had not yet met a philosopher face to face like this, and I
thought of how to prepare myself for this important occasion. Nelson's
Critique of Practical Reason, the first of his three-volume major work
(*Ethics and Pedagogics* and *Theory of Law and Politics* followed later as
the second and third volumes), had just been published. I obtained a copy
and, summoning my courage, started working my way through it, making
copious notes to check whether I had understood.

Reading this book was an extraordinary experience for me, like being
enclosed in a majestic dome, with an organ playing beautiful music. I felt a
captive, overawed yet elated and aware of a never-before sensed freedom. I
remember three main impressions. First, I was sure of having now found
something for which I had been groping in my revolt against the church:
the basis for a view of life and the purposes which should guide it, a view
not dependent on revelation and a supernatural force, nor tied to the
fetters of any dogma, but giving free range to the mind searching for truth.
Secondly, I noted with relief that there was no need to be an expert,
familiar with philosophical terminology, to follow the arguments, which
were presented in crystal-clear structure and lucidly explained. Thirdly,
language and style in their deliberate simplicity (sometimes bordering on
monotony) were so much in accordance with the ideas that the whole had
a striking harmony and beauty of its own.

When I arrived at the Nelsons' home at Eichenallee, I was still in this
mood, but it had vanished when I left. For there had been no contact with

the man who had written the book. Nelson had just sat there, stirring his tea, apparently waiting for me to say something. But despite the powerful impression his book had made on me—or was it because of that?—I felt unable to think of anything worth saying. So I ventured forth with the statement "I have just read your *Critique*"—full stop. Nelson said "Oh", or something to that effect. His charming father ended the embarrassment by talking about Göttingen. This produced on his son's part the confirmation for which I had come: "So I shall see you at Göttingen". I nodded, and left. When, later, I once asked Nelson why he had been so unforthcoming, he tried to explain: "Well, you just seemed to want to stress that you had read the *Critique*—so what was there for me to add?" Nelson was shy, and often awkward; he never liked to engage in small talk for conversation's sake. But with his friends he did not talk only about matters related to common concerns in the work. He would communicate his enjoyment of beautiful things, and also of small pleasures, such as a tasty dish or a hot bath after a journey (in his flat at Göttingen there was no bathroom).

After the first discussion at Göttingen led by Nelson, when I went back to my digs, the feeling of elation returned. It was not the same as when I had been overwhelmed by my solemn impression of a massive systematic intellectual effort; rather, I felt light-hearted and joyous as the result of my first experience of a Socratic discussion in which *we*, the participants, were made to think and express our thoughts clearly and consistently. Our minds were set working, probing, examining assumptions, drawing conclusions, re-examining them when challenged. (An attractive des- cription of Socratic discussions appeared in Nelson's *The Socratic Method,* published in English, with other essays, in 1949 by Yale University Press and Oxford University Press.)

I knew at once that I would gain tremendously by participating in such discussions, that my tools for independent thinking would be sharpened. I also felt that my self-confidence would grow, although I admit that this was not the case with everybody. Some lost confidence because they could not stand being driven into a corner by Nelson's sarcasm, which indeed would run away with him at times, as it also did in his polemical writings when he hit mercilessly at his opponents. I took great pains in writing reports of the discussions in which progress and regress in the arguments as they had gone forward and backward had to be carefully recorded. It was an excellent training of one's analytical powers. I benefited by this training all my life, in teaching, lecturing, writing and especially in editorial work. Sometimes, I remember, we got a little irritated when a report which was read out was challenged next time, and the whole evening went on tracing the mistakes, so that we never reached the next question. And reports of such discussions were particularly difficult to write. Still, even that was useful training.

On the first evening, Nelson had stated and explained the reasons for the conditions to be fulfilled by the participants, as he always did when starting a co-operative effort—even in his university teaching. I thought the conditions, such as punctuality, regular attendance, writing reports, speaking loudly and distinctly, were eminently reasonable. But soon I faced a personal dilemma. The date for the wedding of my sister Lucie had been fixed, and my parents asked me to come to Berlin, sending me the fare. At first, it looked as if I would have to choose between going to Berlin and avoid being absent from one of the discussions. Missing a discussion, I foresaw, would lead to my not being able to continue, but a refusal to attend the wedding would once again upset my family. I am sure that had it been necessary to choose I would have chosen to stay at Göttingen, but I escaped from the dilemma by discovering a helpful train connection. This was one of the early occasions when I was introduced to the consequences of taking commitments seriously.

A few weeks later I learned about another aspect of life in the Göttingen group. I was invited to visit Nelson for a talk. The way in which his very able and devoted secretary Bertha Gysin (who later, when she realised that money for the work was urgently needed, went back to her father's business in Switzerland to earn some) conveyed this invitation made me wonder whether anything had gone wrong. This was indeed the case, though the matter proved not to be serious. The students in Nelson's closer circle who had been there before me had complained about me, expressing doubts about my character. They had felt obliged to include me, the newcomer, in their educational endeavours, but apparently had not known how to approach me directly. Nelson told me without much ado what their complaints were: that I was merely intellectually interested, that I was arrogant, too conscious of being clever (I suspect they may also have thought that I was too aware of being good-looking— Minna Specht often recalled my wearing the becoming pale blue dress, with the pretty Venetian collar, that my mother-in-law had made from dyed bed linen.) In short, they could not really trust me.

Nelson asked me what I thought. I confessed to being at a loss. I was certainly deeply interested intellectually, but "merely"? I knew that I was not attracted only by the logical fireworks, although I enjoyed them greatly. And "arrogant"? Perhaps I was, without being aware of it. I could try to watch it. Confidence, I said, must be mutual and it would take time to grow. Having, rather reluctantly, I thought, done what he considered his duty, Nelson was apparently relieved and we parted in the most friendly manner. His last words were: "Perhaps we should have another talk another time." Never, I thought, not this type of talk anyhow! Nor was it in fact repeated. My relations with the group members improved, especially as a close friendship developed between me and one of them, Elli Neuhaus, a student of medicine like myself.

Usually, when there was a problem of this kind, Nelson's co-worker Minna Specht would deal with it (she was away that summer). Nelson realised that he needed her for the practical application of his ideas, especially in education. My first meeting with Minna took place at about the same time as my first encounter with Nelson. But with her there was an immediate warm contact. At that time, Minna was teaching at a school in the Berlin suburb of Lichterfelde, not far from Dahlem where I lived. I visited her in her ice-cold room. She remained in bed when I came, to keep warm, while I forgot the cold because of the warmth generated inside me by my talk with Minna. A few years later, Nelson entrusted to Minna the responsibility for the *Walkemühle,* the school established to attempt a non-authoritarian education of children, for which the principles can be found in Nelson's *Ethics and Pedagogics.* My daughter, Renate, was in that school for three years. Minna was also in charge of the residential adult college in which young socialists were trained for service and leadership in the political field. My own relations with the *Walkemühle* were those of a friend and active supporter: I found some of the first students for it in the political youth circles in which I worked in Berlin.

In the summer of 1918 I was invited to take part in a one-week course at Göttingen to which not only members of the Göttingen group came, but also people from other towns, teachers, clerical workers, engineers, housewives, a few academics. Previously Nelson had been disappointed with many of his co-workers associated with him in the publication of the Essays of the Fries School of Philosophy because they did not draw from theoretical insights the practical conclusions which he considered compelling. He had therefore started to approach people from other walks of life, and was seeking contact with the Labour movement rather than liberal political circles as he had done before. After the war he himself joined the USPD, and then the SPD.

The course in 1918 was the first course on fundamentals led by Nelson and Minna Specht, which became an annual tradition. It was not an extended Socratic discussion, although some time was set aside for such discussions led by Nelson. The course comprised a series of lectures based on carefully prepared theses; none was given by Nelson. An analysis was presented of the injustices in the world; the organisations and ideologies that upheld them; the need for political action to establish a just state; the form of leadership organisation (leadership was not then as discredited a term as after Hitler) designed to avoid the pitfalls of both autocratic and democratic systems—for the latter, the Weimar Republic, even in its earliest stages, was to offer shocking evidence; education for leadership, i.e. for responsibility in the political struggle and in the wielding of power once power was won; last but not least, the obligations arising for individuals, especially youth, willing to fight for justice—in general terms, meaning the obligation for themselves to refrain from exploitation and to give priority to the demands of the struggle for justice over personal ends.

A rational case was built up step by step, day after day, in an almost dramatic fashion, and every step was open to examination, and was thoroughly discussed. Yet, at the end of the course, the impression was that of a profound emotional challenge. I felt that, not only did I now stand on more solid ground, but also that, come what may, I would not be deflected from the political commitment towards which I had been moving. To put it another way, while in the Socratic discussions I had enthusiastically responded to an intellectual challenge, the course faced me with a moral one, in response to which my convictions as a socialist were reinforced. However, without the intellectual satisfaction I had received in the Socratic discussions, the emotional appeal of the course would probably not have been so strong.

In 1919 I participated again in a similar course, this time as a lecturer for the last session on the subject of individual obligations. I was asked at the last moment to deputise for the speaker who was to deal with this subject, but could not come because she had been refused leave of absence from work. I knew her from the course in 1918, but as far as I remember never saw her again. To my surprise, fifty-four years later in England, I received a letter from her with a large cheque for the Society for the Furtherance of Critical Philosophy, founded in Britain in 1940 by Minna Specht and other supporters of Nelson's ideas. I was touched by her words: "I am one of those who have fallen by the wayside . . .".

The telegram in 1919 with the request to take this friend's place as a lecturer reached me on an island in the North Sea, Amrum, where I was by myself for the last part of a holiday to which my mother-in-law had invited me. I was absorbed in reading Dostoevsky's *Brothers Karamazov,* sitting in a shelter by the sea, with the autumn wind howling around me, and no other human being in sight. With a sigh of regret, I put Dostoevsky on one side, and prepared myself for the lecture and my premature departure.

By the time the second course was held, we were no longer an informal group. We had become organised in the IJB, with local branches, but the centre still at Göttingen. The IJB (*Internationaler Jugendbund,* International League of Youth) was international in aspiration, but its members were in Germany, apart from a few in Switzerland. It was launched in Berlin shortly after the revolution of 1918. How excited we all were in anticipation of appearing for the first time in public, free from the war-time censorship restrictions. What would the response be? The hall was crowded. These were extraordinary times when the public, especially the young people, awakened after the nightmare of the war, were looking for new ideas. It had been arranged that a professional stenographer would take down the proceedings. When Minna Specht saw him sitting by a separate table beside the platform, with twelve sharpened pencils neatly arranged in front of him, she was somehow overawed. "Twelve pencils", she whispered to me, "I have counted them. If we do not succeed tonight, I don't think we ever will."

The striking success of which Minna in her keen imagination had dreamt did not materialise, neither on this occasion nor on similar ones later. Nelson was not a good platform speaker though be could be brilliant in debate. The appeal of his ideas was not instantaneous, not for crowds. In our organisation success always depended on persistent effort and hard work through which we attracted serious people who became members, readers and distributors of publications, supporters of activities we launched, or who gave money for the *Walkemühle* and other purposes without ever attaching strings to their donations.

The IJB was an educational group. Its members at first worked in one or the other of the three Left parties. The Independent Social Democratic Party (USPD), a break-away from the Social Democratic Party (SPD) because of its opposition to the SPD's support of the war, was split in 1920 when the majority joined the Communist Party. The minority was reunited with the SPD in 1922. Those of our members who worked in the Communist Party were not tolerated there for long because they did not fit into its dogmatic autocratic organisation nor did they see any hope for a change in its irresponsible policies. Thus before long we all found ourselves in one party, the SPD, until 1925, when a conflict led to the decision of its Executive to declare membership in the IJB incompatible with membership in the SPD. How did this conflict arise?

Members of the IJB shared the aim which the Labour and socialist movement has proclaimed since its early days: a society free from exploitation and oppression in which the claims to equality and human dignity of all, irrespective of race, class, creed, nationality or sex, are acknowledged and respected. But, as members of the IJB, we stressed the ethical foundations of socialism, anchored in the philosophical concepts of

Kant, Fries and Nelson. This led to some divergence from Marxist tenets traditionally upheld by the party, though criticised also by others within the SPD, Marxists as well as non-Marxists. The emphasis of the IJB was on educating active members who took their ethical convictions and responsibilities seriously. It saw in ideals and the education of those willing to serve them a "better security" (the title of one of Nelson's pamphlets) for the achievement of socialism, meaning a classless and just society, than in the "scientific" analysis of the trends of development in society which, according to Marxian teachings, showed that socialism was the necessary historical outcome.

The basic demands fulfilled by members who took part in this educational endeavour caused me no great difficulties, i.e. to be a vegetarian, cut links with the Church, work actively in a trade union, abstain from drinking alcohol, strive for independence in personal relations, make financial sacrifices. But the concrete tasks which were expected of me were often exacting. An example from my early days in the IJB, when I was back at Göttingen in 1920 for a few months—Nelson asked me to take charge of a course to introduce to its ideas some students attracted to the IJB. This course was a great ordeal for me. I was still very inexperienced in leading discussions. Some of the participants were exceptionally bright, and caused me great embarrassment with their penetrating questions. When I wanted to get on to practical, ethical and political issues (where I felt at home), they continued to dwell on theoretical problems, such as the freedom of will, with which I was unable to cope. Recently, when I talked with one of them now living in New York about those days of our youth, he told me something I had not known then. Taking pity on me, he and the others had agreed among themselves to "behave" and cause me no further agonies. I remember my feeling of relief at somehow having got through, though I was very conscious of my inadequacy.

By undertaking such educational work, the IJB did not place itself outside the framework of the SPD. In fact, it worked loyally within that framework, making no attempt to convert the SPD, for instance, to the leadership idea which it accepted for itself and envisaged for a future "party of reason". Yet its members, by being hard-working, disciplined and devoted, were considered inconvenient, if not dangerous, by some SPD local leaders, when increasingly they won respect in the ranks of the SPD. They aroused hostility, particularly among party officials, because of their support for more radical policies than were pursued by the SPD or by the coalition governments in which it was a partner. Attacks on proposals for a concordat with the Catholic Church, or demands for more energetic measures against right-wing extremists, were cases in point.

Theoretical differences apart, because of such demands on political issues IJB members often sided with Marxist leftists. This was my own experience in the "Young Socialists", an organisation grouping party members between eighteen and, as far as I remember, thirty years of age, to whose national executive committee I was elected. There I worked closely with the Marxist wing, especially in opposition to the so-called Hofgeismar group (Hofgeismar being a place where it had held a conference). This group was against the class struggle, and favoured, instead, ideas of national renewal which recalled some of the romantic aspirations of the pre-1914 *Wandervogel* youth. The ideas of the Hofgeismar group, so we feared, would be grist to the mills of Hitler's emerging National Socialists, and weaken the Labour movement, his main enemy.

To return to the IJB's conflict with the SPD, reports from some local organisations and press publicity directed against the "Nelson Group" caused the national executive of the SPD to invite the IJB for a discussion at its Berlin headquarters in Linden Strasse. I have vivid memories of that meeting in November 1925. I was one of the five IJB representatives, the others being Nelson, Minna Specht, Willi Eichler (then Nelson's secretary) and Max Hodann. It was a memorable meeting, memorable in particular for its unexpectedly abrupt end. Nelson was asked to speak first. He explained the position of the IJB. When he mentioned that he, like other members, had first been in the USPD and then joined the SPD, Crispien, formerly a leader of the USPD, interrupted, shouting in great excitement: "This is untrue—you were never in the USPD, otherwise I would know it!" Nelson calmly asked the Chairman, Otto Wels, to protect him against the insinuation that he was a liar; there would otherwise be no point in continuing. The Chairman would not call his fellow executive member to order, but merely asked Nelson, in a rather impatient tone, to continue. Nelson repeated his request, to no avail. So without a further word, he got up, put on his coat and left the room, followed by the four of us. Willi Eichler gave expression to his indignation by slamming the door so vigorously that it shook the building. After recovering from its amazement, the party executive proceeded to take the decision to expel IJB members.

On the following day Franz Lepinsky, who had been present as representative of the Young Socialists and with whom I was on friendly terms, admitted to me that Crispien had been in the wrong as he could not possibly have known all members of the former USPD, and that Wels should have rebuked him. "But", he added, "you could all still have spoken and perhaps the decision would then have been a different one." This I consider highly doubtful, especially since other groups on the party's left—none of them pro-communist—suffered the same fate. It was my impression that neither Wels nor his colleagues understood why anybody should be so fussy about a point such as the one to which Nelson had taken exception. They did not grasp what was going on in the mind of a man like Nelson, who saw no sense in trying to communicate and cooperate when minimum requirements of fairness were ignored by responsible SPD leaders.

It would be wrong to conclude from the firm moral stand Nelson took on that occasion that he was too unrealistic for politics. It is true that some of his basic ideas, especially concerning democracy and leadership, were unrealistic in the sense that they did not sufficiently appreciate historical background and development. But he, and the organisations he inspired, did adhere to the "ethical realism" they proclaimed. This was acknowledged by a Marxist author, Werner Link, in a book published in Germany in 1964 on the history of the IJB and the ISK (the name adopted after the IJB's expulsion from the SPD). Personally I experienced on several occasions Nelson's insistence on realism in political judgment. Some time in 1924 I lamented in a letter to him the many decisions we had to take in favour of the "lesser evil", for example in elections when none of the candidates seemed to be good and deserve support on positive grounds. I added that I found this situation more and more disgusting. As Minna Specht told me later, Nelson wrote in the margin of my letter: "Would Maria rather choose the greater evil?" Perhaps this was also the sense of the reply I received, but having destroyed all my correspondence before I emigrated in 1933, I cannot confirm this.

Thus in 1926 the IJB, with virtually no loss of members, became the ISK (*Internationaler Sozialistischer Kampfbund*—Militant Socialist International—always referred to by its initials). I remember being glad that ISK became immediately the name used by all, for I felt that the full name was not only heavy but even pompous. We all liked it because it reminded us of *Iskra,* the Russian paper for which Lenin had written—there was still some romantic feeling of sympathy for Soviet Russia among all left groups at that time. *Iskra* meant the spark. The German equivalent was later chosen as the title of our daily paper *Der Funke.* The ISK continued the educational work of its predecessor, the IJB, but it was also a political group, independent of other parties although not putting up its own candidates in elections. As it was,

Plate 1. The Saran Family in 1901. From left to right: Hilde, Kurt, Lucie, Mother, Maria, Father, Grete, Käte, Walter.

[facing p. 50

Plate 2. The Botticelli girl: Maria, aged 19.

Plate 3.

Plate 4.

Plate 5.

Plates 3-5. Maria with Max Hodann, and Renate, born in 1921.

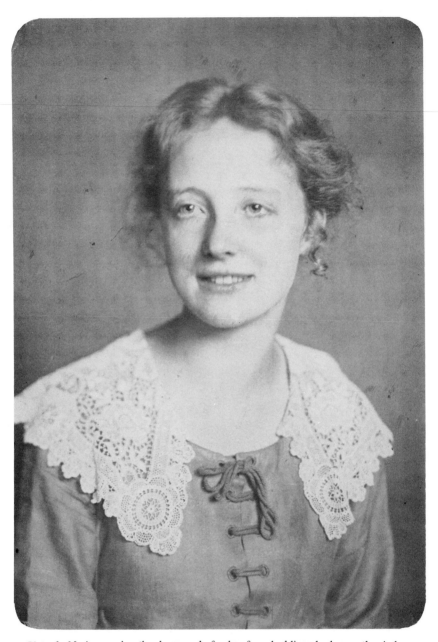

Plate 6. Maria, wearing the dress made for her from bed-linen by her mother-in-law.

Plate 7. Leonard Nelson, from a drawing by his mother.

Plate 8. Max Hodann in 1935.

Plate 9. Renate aged three.

Plate 10. Maria with
Minna Specht.

Plate 11. Willi Eichler
and Minna Specht
(1931).

elections did not increase in importance with the frequency with which they occurred in Germany. They were, however, a barometer for the decline of democracy and the rise of nationalism in the Weimar Republic. It was not surprising that the ISK and other independent groups should have looked for other forms of action to meet the rising danger of Fascism.

My own political life in the second half of the Weimar period was largely determined by the framework of the ISK, by its decisions and activities which reflected our struggle "against all the odds".

Because the ISK consisted of small, compact groups of trained members who trusted each other and had learned to persevere in the face of obstacles and difficulties, it was in many ways better prepared than others for the transition to illegal work after Hitler's seizure of power. The important part it played in the anti-Nazi resistance has been widely acknowledged. Furthermore, thanks to its structure, the ISK was effective and able to wield influence in emigration, in Paris, then in London. It had money, for instance, to issue publications because its members were used to earning money for the organisation. Many of us lived in communities, which was cheaper, in addition to encouraging those who found life in a strange country difficult. Willy Brandt, paying tribute to Willi Eichler a few days after Eichler had died in 1971, stressed his influence as leader of the ISK as a major factor in preparing the way for a united reconstructed SPD after the fall of Hitler.

Leonard Nelson died of pneumonia in 1927 at the early age of 45, having made outstanding contributions in the realms of philosophy, education and the reform of society. Many people then expected the collapse of our organisation. They believed that we acted under Nelson's personal influence as his fanatical followers. This was far from the truth. How it looked to me, I explained in a speech in London on 26 October 1947 at a memorial meeting on the twentieth anniversary of Nelson's death: "His influence was not due to any qualities of his personality but rather to the strength of the impersonal . . . Nelson believed that man can make justice the *main* spring of his actions and therefore wield power not arbitrarily but justly. And he lived his own life in proof of this truth . . . It was from this that I believe his influence sprang. It was impersonal because the demands that spring from reason were decisive."

These memoirs are not the place for a general appreciation of Nelson's work. I mention but one result achieved in Germany long after his death: the Godesberg programme of the SPD adopted in 1959 assigned to the basic ethical values the important place and guiding role denied to them in party programmes in Nelson's time. The main credit for this and for securing the SPD members' understanding belongs to Nelson's disciple Willi Eichler, former Chairman of the ISK, who presided over the drafting committee. Eichler had also been the SPD's representative on the Committee of the Socialist International which drafted the latter's statement "Aims and Tasks of Democratic Socialism" in 1951.

My own life was influenced to no mean degree by Nelson, by his ideas, his way of teaching and the example he set in his own dedicated life. My personal debt to him is not diminished by the fact that on some important questions I came to adopt different standpoints from the conclusions he had reached. The same can be said of most of us who worked with Nelson. We did not feel like an "élite", as we were often accused; we were very conscious of our limitations. But, I admit, we were too sure that we knew all the answers or, in our philosophical outlook, had the basis for discovering them. Experience taught me greater humility. Many problems became even more complex after the Second World War than they had been, or at rate had appeared to us, in the twenties and thirties. Even though the same basic values provide guidance—and I am convinced that this important assumption remains valid—the path of progress towards a more humane society is beset by many more difficulties and uncertainties than we realised when we were young.

VI

Against All the Odds in Weimar Germany

My life and work in Berlin in the latter half of the Weimar era were entirely overshadowed by the decline of the Republic which was steadily gathering speed. I do not intend to add to the existing literature about these fatal years; a full historic record and analysis of events are available. But without a personal account of this part of my life, these memoirs would be incomplete. My vision in looking back is somewhat blurred here, and I have no private papers to which I could turn to clarify the picture. All the time I was aware of the shadows darkening, but I lived as if in a haze.

Outwardly my life continued to follow its course, determined by conditions and convictions. Political activities and my job absorbed me, sometimes to the point of exhaustion. The attacks of migraine from which I had suffered since my childhood were becoming more severe and more frequent. Fortunately, this affliction, with which I had to cope especially at times of nervous strain, disappeared with advancing age.

What sense was there in continuing a struggle which appeared to be more and more hopeless? There was no escaping this vexing question. The grounds for hoping that Hitler's triumph might still be prevented were becoming increasingly slender, as evidence of his growing strength and mad obsessions was becoming ever more formidable. It was desperate to have to witness how his opponents, most important among them the Labour movement, were failing to do what might still have saved the situation. After 1933, the same question became even more vexing for those who engaged in acts of resistance, within Germany, against the totalitarian régime of Hitler. The comrades who resisted then really had *all* the odds against them, as they fought on, dispersed, isolated, constantly endangered.

Much of what was happening in the years preceding the Nazi victory often appeared almost unreal to me. Yet I recall clearly certain experiences of everyday life which illustrate the prevailing atmosphere in Berlin.

In 1928, we—half a dozen ISK members—moved to the Wedding, a working-class district in the north of Berlin, which we considered a more congenial neighbourhood than the Hansa district in the west end where we had lived in a community flat before. When Renate returned from her first outing in the streets with her beloved roller skates, she was in tears crying: "The children here are so rough". On the same day I overheard a conversation outside my window. Someone asked who had moved in there on the first floor. In a rather contemptuous tone of voice someone replied: "Oh, just a tall miss with a child and a few strange young people." So the people of the Wedding did not regard us as congenial newcomers, I thought, at least not to start with.

However, they were solidly against the Nazis. The following incident was typical. One evening there was a commotion at the street corner outside our house in Adolf Strasse (its name a constant hateful reminder of the *Führer's* first name, but given to the street ages before anyone even dreamt of Adolf Hitler). I noticed that people were talking not noisily but in ominous murmurs. I looked out of a front window in our flat. There was a man lying in the middle of the street, unconscious, with blood streaming from his head. He was surrounded at a distance by a crowd of people none of whom made any move to extend a helping hand or let anybody else pass through the circle. I learned that the injured man was a Nazi supporter who, to my own and other people's surprise, lived in the building behind our block. After a political brawl in which he had been involved, he had been left there bleeding. Finally, the police arrived to take him away.

As the government of Germany moved more and more to the right, demonstrations of workers were often broken up. Dispersed segments of marches held in the centre of the city were pursued into our district by mounted police. Like other children Renate learned to hide quickly in a shop, courtyard or house entrance at the sound of those approaching horses.

Generally, our children were coping with problems as they arose, but not worrying overmuch about the gloomy future prospects which preoccupied their elders. Sometimes, however, Renate was worried about my health, or even sensed that I might be in personal danger. In any case she often implored me not to go to a meeting. "I'll telephone the meeting", she would threaten, "and tell them that you are ill." My reply that she did not have a telephone number made her furious but disarmed her. I had to pacify her, which I did, for example, by allowing her to sleep in my bed, where she enjoyed reading by the nice bed lamp on the wall, and to read for as long as she liked. She was a very accommodating child.

All those years she shared my room. Often I had to type there in the evening but she assured me that she did not mind at all; on the contrary the regular sounds of the bell lulled her to sleep. She used to count them, but never got beyond thirty!

Children who live in political circles, especially at a time of stress, become politically aware at a relatively early age. Once Renate, with a few friends, organised a fund-raising occasion in our flat at which they did some play acting. The scenes which they had thought out themselves reflected their observations during the Berlin transport strike in 1932—the famous, or rather infamous, strike called jointly by Nazis and communists against the social democratic administration of Berlin. It was amazing to see how true to life different types of workers and their jargon were portrayed by the children. One of the scenes they performed showed a trial of strikers. There was a moment when we could not help laughing out loud. When the sentence was pronounced, the girl who played the judge wanted to cite a law in support of the sentence, but the only one she remembered was paragraph 218—the law against abortion! It was not surprising that this should come to her mind. The children constantly heard talk about paragraph 218. Opposition to it was then very much to the fore among workers who were embittered by growing mass unemployment but also among middle-class people less economically desperate. Some prominent ladies, for example, were collecting signatures for publication of women who had had abortions, far enough in the past not to be punishable any longer. Later, the Nazis, with their racial obsessions, did not even allow propaganda for the abolition of paragraph 218; at least people they considered "racially pure" should have as many children as possible! The post-war Federal Republic is still meeting obstacles in its present belated attempt at reform, probably because of Catholic opposition.

Several years after we had moved to Britain, Renate—by then Rene—once acted the role of a German Nazi in a play staged by the children of Dora Russell's school which she attended. The way in which she acted the part was very striking. No doubt she was drawing on her still vivid memories of Nazi types—stupid, coarse, arrogant, cheeky.

The police, from whose horses our children knew how to escape, displayed an excess of zeal and even some brutality at times, but there was no need then always to fear them. I knew, for instance, that I could still count on them for protection when threatened by either Nazis or communists, as I often was. I remember one of the last public meetings organised by the ISK in Berlin, jointly with some other left-wing socialist groups. The meeting was broken up under the "emergency laws", which was not unusual in those days. When some phrase or other was used by a speaker to which the invariably present security officer raised objections, he would take it as a reason, or pretext, for intervening. As the people were leaving, slowly and in anger, I noticed one of the young policemen, sadly and with evident reluctance, enforcing the order. His face looked familiar, and then he approached me, addressing me by my name. Years back he had been a student in one of my trade union classes. He told me that he was still a social democrat. "Has it really had to come this, Frau Hodann?" he said. I never met him again, but he may well have been one of those who warned and aided anti-fascists when the Nazi terror started. Until the purge of the police force was completed, there were many who did this, taking a considerable risk.

In the Wedding district, with its solidly anti-Nazi population, it was only in the last few months of the Weimar Republic that groups of Nazis in uniform started making an appearance in pubs with a full display of their emblems. I noticed it on my nightly rounds of pubs with the ISK paper *Der Funke* when to my surprise, after entering a pub, I was greeted by derisive howls instead of the friendly smiles of sympathisers and potential customers, or at worst indifferent stares. I would then sadly register: another pub "taken over" by the Nazis.

One could only take to one's heels in such cases. No discussion was possible or advisable with Nazis. On the other hand, with some communists, individually and informally, one could still talk. For leaders like Willi Münzenberg, the talented communist mass media expert, I personally had a weak spot (I learned later that he met a horrible death on his flight in German-occupied France, betrayed to the Gestapo by a companion). I was never actually attacked but communists would often shout in the street: "We won't let you go home". This happened for instance after a public meeting of the ISK held in a hall in Müller Strasse, one of the main roads in our district, at which I was the speaker. Among the crowds who streamed in we noticed many communist supporters. We sensed that there would be trouble. When half-way through my speech, I reached the question of trade union unity and criticised the Communist Party's policy, pursued since 1929, of splitting the trade unions, the uproar started. The ring-leaders asked everyone to leave the hall in protest. To their surprise, however, only a relatively small number, perhaps a fifth of the audience, joined in the noisy exodus. Our stewards shepherded them out, then locked the doors. When it dawned upon the communists how few had left, they wanted to return. At our request the police, who were waiting nearby, came to guard the doors. The meeting proceeded in good order. One enjoyed these small triumphs.

Proposals for united anti-Nazi action were opposed by the leadership of both the SPD and the KPD. We in the ISK saw the best chances of winning support for such action in trade union circles. Hence I made it my business to attend meetings in different parts of Berlin which seemed to offer an opportunity for speaking in the discussion. The case for genuine united action went often by default, usually because the communists were allowed to dominate the scene unopposed. I had to take my courage in both hands to face their intimidating behaviour.

Our mood might be described as "hoping against hope". But, after the events of July 1932, I admitted, at least to myself, that honestly one could no longer cherish any hope of the catastrophe being averted. I must briefly explain what happened in July 1932.

The Von Papen Government, by *Reich* decree, removed the Prussian government from office, a coalition government led by the social Democrats Braun and Severing. This was an arbitrary, unconstitutional act decided under pressure from the Nazis who at that stage still let others do the dirty work for them, nationalists and reactionaries who were obsessed by fear of the communists or favoured the course towards rearmament they expected from Hitler. Shortly before, this pressure had led to the lifting of the ban on the SA, the Nazis' quasi-military organisation. The ban had been imposed because of the SA's growing provocative terror acts. The Prussian government's removal was rightly seen as getting rid of the major obstacle to giving the SA an entirely free rein and purging the civil service of reliable republicans. It was a kind of clearing operation before the final assault.

The deposed Prussian Ministers did nothing except draft a complaint to the Supreme Court—where it was unlikely even to reach the agenda. The Labour movement looked on. There were protests, but there was no action. This meant that the only remaining bastion of power still available to anti-fascists had been surrendered without any resistance. Undeniably resistance would have involved grave risks, but—of this we, left-wing socialists and others, were convinced—the risks caused by failing to act were even graver. I remember talking soon after these events to some one high up in the police in Kassel whose judgment I trusted. He assured me that even at that late hour effective action would have been possible in Prussia. The police could still be relied upon. The centres of organised Nazi strength could have been broken up; the necessary information and plans were ready to hand, he said, and such action in Prussia—which would have been legal—would have mobilised and solidified opinion against the Nazis in the rest of Germany.

The reactions to the displacement of the Prussian government among my trade union colleagues at work (the Berlin Electricity Works), with whom I was in close contact, were significant, and these were loyal social democrats, critical of my left-wing tendencies. "We are definitely lost, unless we do something now", was their unanimous verdict. Every hour they expected the national social democratic and trade union leaders to issue a call for action. They stayed at their work places throughout the night to be ready for a strike, until it finally dawned upon them that there would be no call. I avoided looking them in the face in the days that followed.

Yet even then I and many others continued being active as before. The idea of giving up before being forced to do so was simply unbearable. We felt that the fact of others having abdicated their responsibility was no valid reason for not holding out to the bitter end.

Two experiences, not important in themselves, show the mood which engulfed us. I decided not to use my three weeks of annual leave in 1932 for the usual kind of holiday—how could one justify a rest at such a time? Instead I went every day to the Insel Strasse offices of *Der Funke* to work for the paper. Several of us who had never had a weapon in our hands took the decision to learn to shoot. Recently, all of a sudden, the memory came back to me of those Sunday mornings we spent on a shooting range in the *Grunewald.* I felt ill at ease, but I put a brave face on the exercise.

In the ISK we continued with our meetings, with our monthly journal the *ISK* published since January 1926 and—in the last year—with our daily paper *Der Funke.* For a small group like ours, many of whose members were unemployed, a daily paper was a tremendous effort in both financial and manpower terms. We had no financial backers except those of us who could afford but small amounts. We paid to all those who worked for the paper on a full-time basis only their modest living expenses. Our school, the *Walkemühle,* was closed to set teachers and students free for political efforts. We organised the publication of an "Urgent Appeal" signed by prominent people from various walks of life and of different political persuasions who agreed on the need to stem the fascist tide. I remember Einstein, Käte Kollwitz, Erkelenz among the signatories. Large posters were displayed all over Berlin on hundreds of the usual advertising pillars.

Der Funke was prohibited for four weeks in November/December 1932 because of an editorial which called Hindenburg a "Protector of Fascism". In fact, he was precisely that, even though early that year he had been elected President of the Republic against the rival candidacy of Hitler. The ISK had then tried in vain to win support in the Labour movement and beyond for a broadly based agreed anti-fascist candidate. The SPD decided in favour of Hindenburg, considering him the only remaining defence against fascism. The KPD maintained the candidacy of its own Thälmann. Hindenburg received nearly nineteen million votes; Hitler more than eleven million; Thälmann five million. We thought that the farce to which democracy in the Weimar Republic had been reduced could hardly go further. In the ISK we had often recognised the need to support the "lesser evil" among candidates or government policies. For instance we had argued for supporting the conservative Brüning government in 1931 when this still meant in effect to keep the Nazis out of the government. On the occasion in 1932 we decided to vote for Thälmann, realising clearly that this was a mere gesture of protest. We could see no real difference at that stage between Hindenburg and Hitler as Presidents, since Hindenburg could be expected to open the front door to Hitler—which before long he did.

Der Funke resumed publication until it was finally banned early in 1933, shortly before the *Reichstag* fire which became the signal for the start of Hitler's terror régime. I remember the morning after the fire when the news came over on the radio. Renate, having answered a ring at our front door bell, came back, flustered with excitement, saying: "Nobody there, but a big parcel in white paper has been left—don't touch it, it is probably a bomb." Remembering the news she had heard just before, she added: "And my father has been arrested!" The paper contained flowers for me. Who could be so crazy as to send flowers on a day like this? They came in fact from a slightly crazy woman who was then pursuing me with her unwanted attentions.

Looking back on the work we did in the ISK between 1925 and 1933 I feel no regrets. We did in the end go down like the rest of Hitler's opponents, but we went down fighting for policies which, as has been widely recognised since, were relevant to the needs of the time: on the economic crisis and the political power situation. Tragically these were not in good hands with either the Social Democratic or the Communist Party.

VII

Social Worker in Berlin

From 1926 to 1933 I was employed as a social worker in the Berlin Electricity Works, Bewag for short. After 1918, the Bewag had been transformed from a municipal into a mixed enterprise to attract private investment. But the City of Berlin, as the main shareholder, still influenced labour conditions. Heinrich Schäfer, the managing director in charge of the personnel section for manual workers (as customary, white-collar workers were is a separate section) was a former trade union organiser and social democratic city councillor. He had new ideas on labour relations for which he won the support of the company directors. Among the innovations was the employment of a social worker; furthermore the establishment of a works school providing classes free of charge on technical, commercial and a few other subjects. Individual employees as well as the firm were to benefit by this institution. It was hoped that, through the new relationship between staff members as teachers and wage and salaried workers as students, the atmosphere on the shop floor and in the office would improve. The management were anxious to show that they had no intention of exercising control from above in a new form. Thus attendance was entirely voluntary, and the school was founded and run in co-operation with the Works Council and the trade unions.

My appointment as a social worker, as well as tutor at the works school, was therefore part of an interesting scheme. Yet I was conscious of a basic problem. As a social worker, I was to deal with cases of personal and family need and the distribution of welfare funds. But I believed in the principle of social insurance and welfare benefits being the concern of public bodies. They should apply to all citizens alike irrespective of such fortuitous circumstances as their place of employment. Moreover, it seemed undesirable to increase the personal dependency of workers on their firm. In Germany, as in other parts of the industrial world, the trend of development was in the direction I favoured, but many schemes were still in operation run by private charities or firms. Since this could not be

60

changed overnight it seemed sensible to make the best of the situation. In any case, it seemed preferable that a social worker should handle such provisions in an enterprise rather than clerks in a routine bureaucratic way, as had been done in the Bewag before.

My subjects at the Bewag school were public health and hygiene. I had been dealing with similar questions in my work in adult education, especially in trade union classes. Most of those who joined the Bewag classes were newcomers to adult education; few would probably have come to a class organised by the trade unions. It was gratifying to reach out to new groups. One class which I particularly enjoyed teaching comprised cleaners at head office, all of them women, who finished their work before office hours began and then came straight to the class. The visits I arranged for them to health and social institutions in Berlin aroused their special interest. They enjoyed being treated on these occasions as honoured citizens entitled to full explanations.

Among other educational functions assigned to me was a summer school for Bewag apprentices. It was a tough job trying to interest teenagers who were sceptical about this type of activity. This was more difficult than dealing with socialist or trade union youth groups, as I had done before, where a certain common interest could be assumed. I accepted modest results as the best that could be achieved.

I had been lucky to be accepted for the position at the Bewag without professional training and a social work diploma. My medical studies, my experience in teaching adults and my close connections with the trade unions had counted in my favour. Since at that time I no longer belonged to the SPD, the party which predominated among the Bewag trade unionists, this might have presented a problem. In the event, I was merely told that I would have to keep my political views, which were to the left of the SPD, outside my sphere of work. This was a fair request, and I never had any difficulties on account of my political affiliation with the ISK. On the contrary, and to my surprise, it was not long before Works Council members and others would ask me for a copy of the *ISK* on the first of the month, and be disappointed if the journal was not yet out.

Bewag workers followed the activities in which I was engaged outside working hours with considerable interest. Sometimes they were bewildered by what their respected social worker was apparently up to. As I was known to many in the Bewag, news spread quickly about my having addressed a meeting, being mentioned in the press, having canvassed door to door in one or other political cause or sold political literature outside meetings and in pubs, as we used to do night after night when the need for action against the Nazi threat became more and more pressing. One morning, the lift attendant at Bewag headquarters, where I had my office, greeted me on my arrival by saying in a hushed voice: "Excuse me, but we have been wondering, are you so badly paid that you must sell papers at night?"

The managing director Heinrich Schäfer, when he interviewed me, had warned me sternly against political proselytising. As a relationship of confidence developed between us, we often talked about political issues after settling matters concerning my work. The last such discussion in his room was memorable. Hitler had seized power; the Nazi flag had just been hoisted on the Bewag buildings; we had learned that we were both among the first dismissed on political grounds. Schäfer's comments were that the Nazis would not be able to govern for long, since they would make a mess of things; they could not solve the economic problems resulting from capitalism. His belief, rooted in Marxist ideas which he had absorbed since his early days in the Labour movement without ever being a theoretician, was unshaken: even the most serious setbacks were temporary, and could not, in the long run, prevent the victory of the workers' movement. Yet, as we sat there, at that moment of suspense between two historical eras, both of us knew that the immediate future was dark and menacing.

Schäfer, as I remember, strongly advised me to leave Germany, and saw to it—perhaps this was his last move as a director—that I was paid my salary for the next three months at once. The Company Director, Dr Kaufmann, willingly signed the order. His dismissal as a Jew followed a few weeks later, and he then emigrated too. Schäfer remained in Berlin, unmolested at first, cultivating a piece of land (he was a gardener by trade) and trying to keep out of harm's way. He told me this when I saw him again fifteen years later on my first return visit to Berlin after 1933. With his old frankness, he related to me in detail how he had fared. Pressures and threats from the Nazi side had steadily mounted until, in the end, he had given way and signed a membership form for the Nazi party, in order to protect his family. His son, he told me with pride, had managed to avoid army service by wounding himself in the arm, choosing to become a cripple rather than fighting for Hitler in the war. He himself had to stand trial after 1945 before a commission set up by the reestablished SPD. When all the circumstances had been examined he was cleared, which meant readmission to membership of the party. He had then been able to obtain a management position in a small firm, though not in the Bewag.

To return to pre-Nazi days, my experience of working in a big industrial concern was important for me irrespective of the particular work for which I was employed. Previously I had been a socialist intellectual, a teacher, lecturer, public speaker, political activist in the Labour movement. Now I was for the first time working at a centre of economic activity which determined the lives of thousands of people. I was able to gain first-hand impressions of conditions and problems with which I was familiar in general terms. I remember feeling almost thrilled by being an integral part of a large unit, with a place in its hierarchy, sharing practical interests with work colleagues, being active as one rank-and-file trade unionist among others. Soon I was elected as a works representative to an all-Berlin trade union delegates' body, again a new kind of experience for me. All the time, I was conscious of gaining solid ground under my feet.

I had not been working in the Bewag for long when the sudden death of Leonard Nelson, founder and leader of the educational and political movement to which I belonged, faced me with a dilemma. Few ISK members were working in the field of critical philosophy, on the theoretical foundations laid by Nelson. His concern for promoting the application of his ethical ideas in education and politics had led Nelson to put his own theoretical work second. As a result, he had lost some of his academic associates and friends. He had alienated many by his insistence on demands outside the philosophical sphere which they were not willing to accept. The question put to me by Minna Specht after Nelson's death was whether I would transfer my main effort to philosophy even though I was not professionally trained in this field, and would have to study hard. To accept the suggestion would have meant a drastic change in the course of my life for which I was not prepared. Still, I considered carefully the pros and cons before I decided to say no. The work I had started in the Bewag, far from being merely a way of earning my living, was adding something to my development which I felt to be essential. I also felt that it was increasing my usefulness for the political struggle. But an even more weighty reason for my decision was my uncertainty about being able to make a worthwhile contribution in the realm of philosophy.

In addition to experiencing how a large industrial organisation functions, my contact with workers' families deepened my understanding of practical economic and social problems in people's daily lives.

One of the first tasks assigned to me was the distribution of an emergency fund launched by the Bewag to help families of those injured during the construction of its power station *Klingenberg* which had just been completed. This technical masterpiece was attracting scores of visitors from all parts of the world. No glory was reflected in what I was called upon to do. I was in fact dealing out "conscience money" designed to compensate for the loss of life and damage to health suffered by workers employed on the building site. Many accidents had happened. Too many? Impossible to prove such an assertion, but the rate was high. I did not doubt that those in charge had concentrated on the modern wonder they were creating and on the speedy completion of the work. I found that among those whom I met, people with knowledge of the accidents, the air was thick with bitterness and suspicion. They did not believe that sufficient care had been taken; in their view, there had been a lack of concern for human beings.

The part of my regular work which was personally most rewarding was sending children of Bewag employees for recreation to residential homes which I was free to choose. When I could afford the time I accompanied such groups on their journeys. I enjoyed the contact with the children and with those to whose care I entrusted them.

The German economy was still flourishing when I started working at the Bewag. After 1929 the depression caused conditions to go from bad to worse. Nobody who in those years witnessed the long columns of the unemployed of Berlin marching in the biting east wind of a frosty November day to commemorate the 1918–1919 revolution in Germany and, often, also the 1917 revolution in Russia, will forget the picture of misery and despair they presented. There was hardly a flicker of revolutionary spirit or hope to be seen on the faces of these demonstrators. That spirit had died in the frustrations of little more than a decade of the Weimar Republic.

Bewag workers, too, were affected by dismissals and early retirement with meagre pensions. Those who remained in work could count themselves lucky, but even they often suffered from the recession. Many had to support relatives who were out of work and receiving inadequate unemployment benefits, or teenage children unable to find jobs or apprenticeship places. Many families got into debt. Applications to the Bewag management for advances on wages or outright support steadily increased. Loans were rarely of much help, although no interest was charged, for the deductions from subsequent pay packets usually caused new problems.

One aspect of the situation with which I became familiar was the move of families to their allotments on the outskirts of the city. These "garden colonies", as they were called, surrounded much of Berlin. On small pieces of land which cost little rent workers used to grow a few vegetables, fruit, and flowers; rough sheds had been erected on many allotments which served as a shelter on rainy days. Now, with great patience and skill, primitive sheds were converted into some sort of dwelling. It was against the law to live there, and the health of family members certainly suffered in the winter. But the extra income, however modest, derived from letting others use their town flats was an essential part of the budget for many families. It became a problem for me to trace addresses for my visits to the homes of employees, although many workers would inform me confidentially of the location of their allotment. Even so, the directions given were often difficult to follow.

It was then that I discovered the Berlin of the allotment dwellers. Many years later, when I visited the *favelas* of Brazil and the shanty towns of other developing countries, when I saw the "pavement dwellers" of Indian cities, unashamedly so described even in official announcements or the press, I sometimes thought back to my impressions of the Berlin allotment dwellers. I had not then imagined that I would one day see living conditions infinitely worse than the worst in Berlin. Yet for an industrialised country like Germany, with many decades of economic and social progress behind it, they were bad enough to speed the advance of Hitler to power and make people praise him when he abolished unemployment through rearmament.

As the economic crisis deepened and the unemployed approached the six million figure (nearing eight million by 1933 according to some estimates), it became increasingly hard to advise or help effectively in individual cases. However, I had no time to ponder this overmuch. There was a general problem which preoccupied me as it did others. The problem was how to rally the anti-fascist forces to which the Labour movement had to give a lead in that fateful period; how to promote an economic policy to fight the depression—Sweden was beginning to show the way, not by rearmament but, anticipating Keynes, by creating mass purchasing power; and how, even at that late hour, to stem the Nazi tide and prevent the world war which it threatened to unleash.

PART TWO

VIII

Leaving Berlin and Danish Interlude

As an active socialist I faced the choice when Hitler seized power either to emigrate or to stay come what may—that is, if in the first wave of arrests the freedom to choose had not been taken away from me. It was then fairly easy to leave Germany if one had a valid passport and enough money for the ticket. To stay meant continuing the struggle by whatever means were available or could be devised. To leave also meant to continue the struggle, but from the outside. I did not foresee how difficult it would be to mobilise forces against Hitler not only inside but also outside Germany. On the other hand, I was conscious of the dangers of illegal work. Those with whom I was associated had no illusions about the nature of the Hitler régime, even if it might take a little time to get fully into its murderous stride. We had read Hitler's *Mein Kampf* and studied fascist methods at close quarters.

Even in the socialist ranks there were those who did no more than try to survive. Some merely withdrew into as much of a personal life as the régime would allow. Others lived for the day after Hitler whose boast of a "thousand-year Reich" impressed only a few. Comrades with weak nerves were not encouraged to take part in illegal activities since this involved too many risks not only to themselves but to others. Looking back I believe that all Jewish comrades should have left Germany as soon as possible. We did not fully realise how much worse would be their fate compared with that of non-Jews in the same circumstances. As it was, many Jewish socialists stayed to participate in the underground struggle. A few of them, when in immediate danger of arrest, were still able to leave Germany right up to the outbreak of war in 1939. Rescue operations of this kind were possible because some of us had emigrated at an early stage.

This consideration played a part in my decision to emigrate. The likelihood of an early arrest was a factor, too. By agreement, my name was one of those freely to be used by group members when

69

necessary to mention names of associates in Gestapo interrogations, because I would by then be out of the reach of the Gestapo. Such kinds of agreement had been reached in advance of Hitler coming to power, since we knew that, in that event, the previous channels for consultation would not be available, and the liaison network of underground contacts would take some time to establish.

Thus I knew more or less definitely in advance that I would emigrate. I favoured Britain, which I had liked on my visit in 1924, and I was never to regret this choice. The Reichstag fire, even if not provoked by the Nazis as now seems likely, was eagerly seized by them as the pretext for starting the full-scale terror they had long been planning. We knew then that Hitler had arrived. I still remained in Berlin for a few days to settle my affairs as far as possible. But I did not sleep at my own home, nor enter it even by day. Some who failed to observe this rule of elementary caution at that time paid dearly for it. The urge to go home, just to pick up some belongings perhaps, even if acute danger is involved, is amazingly strong. I was not much attached to property and owned little. Thus I had no difficulty in leaving everything behind, taking only a small bag with me. I was lucky, however, in having some of my personal things, even books, brought to London later by friends.

My last night in Berlin was spent at the flat of a retired Bewag worker whom I had known and trusted for many years. He seemed so reliable to me and, being ill, was so little known in his district, that I recommended him later to René Bertholet, a Swiss comrade, who actively supported the illegal work of the ISK in Germany. On one of the occasions when René stayed at that flat he was arrested, together with the Bewag worker himself; both had been denounced to the Gestapo by the latter's wife. I was deeply shocked when I learned about the circumstances of René's arrest. This was two-and-a-half years later, after his release from prison. What had caused this betrayal? Monetary reward? The wife had often been in financial difficulties. Or a suppressed hatred of her sick husband? I never found out. This kind of experience was not unusual in the Hitler days, but our group prided itself on the special care with which it organised its activities.

Shortly before I was due to leave Berlin, I walked with two of my comrades, Willi Eichler and Fritz Grob, in the streets of a North Berlin district to talk things over. They then agreed to go with me as far as the Saarland, leaving it open whether they would return. No entry in the passport, which would have made return more difficult, would be made on the frontiers of the Saar with either Germany or France, under the special status laid down for that industrial region in the Versailles Treaty—a status soon to be abolished by one of Hitler's early "coups".

In the quiet home of our hospitable friend, a Protestant clergyman in the small town of Völklingen, we were able to watch for a while what was happening in Germany, trying to sort things out, digesting news of who had been arrested, making plans for the new era we were entering. In between, I remember, Willi and I took time off to see a Greta Garbo film at Saarbrücken. Then my friends, apparently not threatened by arrest at that time, returned to Berlin to explore the possibilities for illegal work and for the necessary liaison both within Germany and between the Germans and friends in other countries. Willi Eichler later emigrated to Paris which, for our group as for others, became the main centre from which socialist refugees maintained their connections with Germany. Shortly before the war, London took the place of Paris in this respect. Fritz Grob, a pattern maker by profession, who had experience of "going underground" in the First World War when he was a conscientious objector, took up illegal work in Berlin. He was caught after a few years, but survived his years in prison.

My own way went from the Saar via France to Britain. However, I had hardly extended my first feelers there when I was called to Denmark on a special "mission" and left London for Copenhagen.

My mission was to prepare the way for Minna Specht to reopen her school which had been confiscated by the Hitler régime. The new start was to be on a relatively small scale. Mainly those children whose parents had become refugees or did not want their children to be educated in Nazi Germany, though they themselves had decided to stay, would be reassembled in Denmark. The *Walkemühle,* the name of the school in Germany, had also included an adult college for political education which, however, had ceased to function as early as 1931 to enable teachers and students to put all their energies into the fight against Hitler.

In Denmark I had many contacts, having visited the country frequently over the years. I was sure that I could count on old friends for support, and I was not disappointed. My knowledge of the Danish language was useful in tackling my mission. I had not sought this postponement of my own new start in Britain, but I welcomed the breathing space offered, especially the chance of working with Minna, with whom I had been closely linked since 1917.

It was not difficult to find Danish people interested in progressive, anti-authoritarian educational experiments, and to arouse their sympathy. With their help, the necessary official steps were taken. Then the search for a house began. This gave me a chance to visit parts of Denmark I had not seen before, and I appreciated the opportunity. One day in the Isle of Fyn stands out in my memory. It was my birthday, but I had not thought of this at all. At a small station I asked a Dane how to get to the place I intended to see, and he offered to show me the way. When, eagerly chatting, we passed his own cottage, he invited me in for coffee. His family greeted me warmly and, with true Danish hospitality, offered coffee and pastries. As we sat down at table, I remembered the date and told them they were giving me a birthday party. They were delighted, and we parted as friends.

Throughout my life such chance encounters have made me happy, reassuring me of the common humanity which exists not only in songs and proclamations but in reality, everywhere. In 1933 such reassurance meant more than ever.

The house chosen was at Möllewangen, in the north of the Isle of Zealand, near the sea. One of the *Walkemühle* teachers, Gustav Heckmann, came and approved the choice. He was able to bring with him my daughter Renate, whom I had left behind in Berlin. School holidays had just started, which made it easy for her to obtain a children's travel document. When she had gone to the police station with a friend to apply for this document, she overheard one of the police inspectors saying "But her father is in prison", to which his colleague replied "Don't make a fuss". The local police had evidently not yet been purged of "unreliable" elements. Here she was, and her first words whispered into my ears were: "It was wonderful, there was no Nazi in our compartment". It took her a little time to adjust to the happy state of freedom still prevailing in Denmark. She was welcomed into one family, then another, where there were children of her age and where she could stay until our departure for London.

Then Minna joined me in Copenhagen, and we bought the necessary things for the school. She enjoyed satisfying her passion for shopping, but it had to be on a modest scale, since the school's finances were as uncertain as everything else in our lives. Most precious was the brand-new bicycle, a gift from my old friend Rammel, owner of a chain of bicycle shops, whom Minna had asked about a second-hand one she might buy. Denmark being a country where the old and the young invariably ride bicycles, she was at once determined to acquire this skill regardless of her 54 years of age. As soon as we had reached Möllewangen, she began practising, and, after a few days, we were able to cycle together, exploring the nearby woods.

Dusting, scrubbing and decorating took up most of our time; the place had been uninhabited for a considerable period. We preserved elderberries found in the garden, harvested nuts, established the first relations with neighbours, secured wood, potatoes and other provisions for the winter. Here I had to act as interpreter, but we started at once with Danish lessons. Every night we sat by an oil lamp while I taught Minna Danish and she taught me to knit socks. I found that knitting socks soothed my nerves, and I continued this later as a hobby, though only in holiday time.

Our walks towards the evening were always eventful. We enjoyed glorious sunsets by the sea and the autumn colours of the forest. We picked up small useful items which found their way into the pails we were always carrying: pieces of wood from a building site, fruit from the footpaths between the abandoned summer bungalows of Copenhagen families, edible fungi on which Minna was an expert—she infected me with her delight at discovery, and I acquired another hobby, as did my daughter later. (A third one originated in that period: I learned to play bridge from my hosts in Copenhagen.)

We lived in this way at Möllewangen until the children arrived, just the two of us, in simple, beautiful surroundings, in a peace which almost hurt after the horror, fears and tensions we had gone through. When the postman came, dark clouds always shrouded our horizon. News about the fate of friends in Germany reflected the terror raging there. What sense was there in continuing educational endeavours which might be destroyed again by hostile forces? This question was never far from our minds as we followed developments in the world from our quiet corner. But since no action was without risks, the only possible course was to minimize them as far as possible. Minna put all her energies into the new beginning, as she did once again years later when the menace of war in which Denmark might be overrun by Hitler compelled her to leave and seek refuge for her by then enlarged school in Britain. In 1940 the school was uprooted once more by the mass internment of German refugees, fascists and anti-fascists alike, caused by the threat of a German invasion. After 1945, Minna attempted no new start but returned to Germany as head of the famous *Odenwald* school, and later to work in Hamburg for a UNESCO commission.

My memories of those weeks in Denmark in the summer and autumn of 1933 belong to those I particularly cherish. I wrote about them in my contribution to a book published in 1959 for Minna's eightieth birthday. Shortly before her death in 1961, when I saw her in Bremen for the last time, she spoke about my chapter, which was entitled "Pause before a new Start", and her own fond memories of that period. The following quotation indicates the importance of the Danish interval for me at that stage in my life:

"How good it was to have this breathing space before starting a new life with new challenges. While tackling together a necessary practical job, we became deeply conscious of the continuity of the ideas which were shaping our lives. In years filled to the brim with problems, arguments, conflicts, moral demands, disappointments and refusals to capitulate, I had known Minna's stimulating, generous, often disquieting, then again conciliatory personality. At Möllewangen I was wholly at one with her without words, happy in our simple daily tasks, living in a harmony such as I have rarely experienced."

IX

Taking Roots in Britain

On 15 October 1933, I set foot again on the British shore, this time accompanied by Renate, who was soon to become Rene. From the start I wanted to become integrated into British life; an emigrant's existence, dominated by the longing to go back and by reminiscences of the past, never attracted me. And who could predict then how long Hitler would last? Moreover, my British comrades expected me to co-operate with them.

How easy, or how difficult, was it for me to settle down? Compared with many other refugees, it was easy enough. The problem of providing care and education for Rene was greatly eased by the support of people whom I had not even known previously. First it was Dora Russell, who offered a free place for Rene at the residential school which she had founded with Bertrand Russell and was continuing on her own after they had separated. Pending her start at that school, Rene spent a short period at Canterbury in a typical English middle class family with the typical English name Smith, where she could start getting to grips with language and customs. In Berlin she had had a rather unconventional upbringing. Now that we were poor foreigners, often not too welcome perhaps, I impressed on her the need for observing customs even if she did not find them sensible. This was not easy for her. She had always been stubborn in refusing to say things which she did not honestly believe to be true. British people, she now found, were even more attached to formal polite phrases than the Germans, whom she had been allowed to defy. They were constantly saying "sorry", when they did not feel sorry at all, or "thanks ever so much", when gratitude was far from their minds. When, at her first dinner in the Canterbury family, Mrs Smith filled her plate with food, as she did for everybody else, she was startled by Rene's instant reaction: "How can you know how much I want to eat?" Our hostess admitted that Rene had a point there; yet one could not expect everybody to be so understanding. We both learned that it was not the done thing to take the

75

last sandwich or cake from a plate offered. Nor should one talk about food during a meal (the war with its food shortages changed this as many other things).

I was given advice, too, for instance never to mention the fact that I was divorced. I was assured that with no husband in sight I could rely on being taken for a widow and that there would be no embarrassing personal questions. What a contrast to Germany! However, I realized that I need not accept at its face value all the advice offered by Mrs Smith and others. I found out, for example, that British people often appreciated personal frankness, even though they themselves would shy away from it.

In her first weeks at Dora Russell's school, Rene probably suffered some home sickness. This was indicated by the way in which she was frantically possessive about the toys she had brought with her. She cried bitterly when the other children, pulling her leg, hid them from her. Peggy Wilson, the matron, comforted her. When after only two months Rene came to London for her Christmas holidays, she seemed happy enough and already preferred to converse with me in English. She soon almost forgot her German, but got back into it easily when, during the war, she stayed with a group of German friends, and from then onwards, kept it up.

The second generous offer of support for Rene's education—after she had left Dora Russell's school—came from the Chances, who wanted a companion for their youngest daughter of the same age as Rene. The two girls attended the public school at Winchester as day pupils. A public school! This was not the type of school I would have chosen, but beggars cannot be choosers. I was confident, and was proved right, that Rene would not be greatly affected either by public school élitism or the wealthy atmosphere of the Chances' home in the country (butler and all).

Janet Chance and I had some interests in common. We co-operated on several occasions in campaigns for abortion law reform, a field in which I had been active in Germany, and she was one of the leading pioneers in Britain.

At first it was suggested that I should provide for Rene's clothes, and I readily agreed. But when I discovered what the school uniforms, which were obligatory, would cost, I had to confess that this was as much as I had to live on for several months. The subject was quietly dropped, and never mentioned again. Rene spent three happy years in that family, treated truly like a daughter. Janet Chance became a sponsor for Rene's naturalisation, the second one being Graham Hutton, the economist, a friend of the Chance family. After Rene's matriculation, Clifford Chance offered to finance her university studies, as he did for his own daughter. But Rene could not decide on a subject and was really not ready for academic work. For this reason I advised her against accepting the offer. Instead she gained some practical work experience, in a salad kitchen, in Minna Specht's school helping with the children; then, after a training in shorthand and typing, in various offices. Thus she was economically independent before she reached the age of eighteen.

After the war, with her intellectual interests awakened, especially during the period when she was Rita Hinden's secretary at the Fabian Society's Colonial Bureau, she went to Ruskin College, Oxford, for a two-year diploma course, and then studied for a degree in modern history in Manchester, obtaining local and state scholarships for her studies. After graduation in Manchester she became a tutor at Hillcroft College for Working Women at Surbiton, Surrey, taught in evening adult education classes, worked as an editorial assistant for the journal *Socialist Commentary* under its editor Rita Hinden, and after acquiring a PhD became a senior lecturer in Political Thought at the City of London College (later called Polytechnic).

Among the British friends who welcomed me in London in 1933 was Amy Moore, a tutor in psychology for the Workers' Educational Association, of working-class background. She belonged to the small group connected with the ISK in Germany, which became known as the Socialist Vanguard Group. Amy was my standby in many of the initial difficulties I encountered, and the main source of information about the intricacies of the British political scene. Eager as I was to absorb this information in the shortest possible time, her Yorkshire accent was a considerable obstacle, made worse by her rapid speech and her habit of bending down her head while talking. I suffered agonies, but had to get used to it. One could not but love Amy, one of the most selfless and courageous socialists I ever met, and with such a wonderful sense of humour. She died in May 1945, on the day when the Allied victory and the end of the war were announced.

My impressions of the place at Malden Crescent where Amy lived are unforgettable. Since her address included Chalk Farm as the district, and since I had heard that it was near Swiss Cottage, I had a vague notion beforehand of something green and pleasant. How different reality was became clear to me and Rene when Amy took us home for supper after our arrival from Denmark. The small room, which Amy shared with her younger sister Edith until Edith moved to the north, was full of steam. George Green, another group member (later to become general secretary of the Civil Service Clerical Association), was sitting on the floor cooking chips on a tiny gas ring. Why was the kitchen not used instead? One look at it provided the answer. The filth of many years which had accumulated there would deter anybody—except perhaps Amy in her shortsightedness, who, in any case, could ignore outer circumstances, when occupied with important things, better than anyone else I have known. It was indeed hopeless to try to clean up that kitchen. It belonged to Mr Humphries, the owner of the house at Malden Crescent, an intriguing person. He had let the Moores have their room free of rent on the understanding that they would share their dinner with him on Sundays. On the groundfloor he had installed a printing workshop where he and his friends would produce their anarchist publications in their spare time.

Mr Humphries gave Edith and George access to his workshop where they printed leaflets on various occasions, for instance for the left-wing First-of-May Committee of which George was the secretary. George had learned setting and printing at school, and he taught Edith, who became a skilled craftswoman, moving her slim long fingers with a speed which greatly impressed Rene when she watched her. Later the group collected money to buy some type, advised and helped by its Sheffield member, Joe Johnson, a printer who instructed Edith in lay-out. Its journal, the *Vanguard,* later *Socialist Vanguard*—which in 1942 became *Socialist Commentary*—was then set by her for several years to save money. Edith liked to tell how she used to redraft sentences when she ran out of a certain letter, searching for words which would not contain this letter. In London the type was kept under the bed or, rather, beds, for because of lack of space one bed had to be pushed underneath the other in day time.

There was something romantic and a little bizarre about that place at Malden Crescent and some of the people who went in and out there. But Rene, on our first evening, saw only its slummy condition and asked me with a deep sigh: "Are we to live like this in Britain?" Well, we did not, even though we lived simply. I do not remember, for example, having a proper wardrobe before 1945, instead of some hooks in a corner, to hang up clothes. This was a minor inconvenience when one had few clothes to hang up anyhow.

Where was I to live and how would I earn my living? By a stroke of luck a small legacy had fallen due which my sister Hilde had been able to send to me in Denmark just before such transfers were entirely forbidden. It was enough to face the first few months and, what was more important, to open a bank account. This, I learned, was essential for any official dealings; without a reference from your banker you could not get far in Britain. I was even lent some additional money to pay into my account so that I might achieve greater, and more enduring, "trustworthiness".

In my search for accommodation my first intention was not to burden myself again with furniture having just abandoned everything in Berlin to an unknown beneficiary. But after seeing the unbelievably horrible furnished rooms in the Camden area available at rents I could contemplate, I quickly changed my mind. Unfurnished rooms, even in neighbourhoods less dismal than the one I had explored in Camden, were relatively cheap; so was second-hand furniture. Some things could be obtained from families well-disposed towards us newcomers. Susie and Elsie, connected with our group through their teacher in an East European country, a follower of Nelson's philosophy, had recently arrived to study, or work, in London. Together we took three attic rooms in Englands Lane, Hampstead, and procured the necessary furniture and equipment. George, always helpful and inventive, fixed a shelf for a gas burner on the landing for us; further down there was a toilet with a wash basin. My main memories of this my first London home are of shivering in the exceptionally cold winter; of struggling to light the open fire to which we were not accustomed (probably the chimney had not been swept, so even fortunes spent on firewood did not help much); of being in fear of our landlady, who lived on the floor below and who might give us notice if we made a nuisance of ourselves. Yet this was precisely what we did.

There was the day when Susie's apron went up in flames while she was standing with her back to the open fire, which, for once, was burning brightly. We had been collating a manuscript by Ernst Toller, which I had typed in ten copies and spread out on the bed. With great presence of mind, Susie grabbed a blanket from underneath the typed pages, wrapped it round herself and rolled on the floor to extinguish the flames. Then I noticed that the blanket had started smouldering and quickly fetched some water. But when I opened the door the landlady smelt the smoke, and I had to reassure her as best I could. My first concern, I must admit, was to save the typed pages, but before long I dashed down to the chemist for first aid to dress Susie's burns.

Another day, Elsie, to whom mishaps often happened, sent several empty milk bottles waiting to be taken outside the front door, rolling down the two flights of stairs with a deafening clatter. What a commotion! It was really funny, but the landlady apparently did not think so.

One night when I came home late, I had forgotten my keys. The girls were still up, their windows showed light. But I did not dare to ring the bell nor to shout loud enough for them to hear (I never could whistle). So I walked to Malden Crescent which was not far, woke up Amy, and crept into her bed; no need to fear her landlord, the friendly anarchist.

Typing manuscripts was one means of earning some money; another was helping out as a waitress at the Vegetarian Restaurant near Leicester Square opened by Jenny and Walter Fliess, German ISK members. At a time of mass unemployment, few jobs were available for foreigners. Sometimes we pursued crazy ideas. Susie had met a charming sculptor whom she had tried to interest in my profile as a desirable object for his art. I suppose I was somewhat flattered by her suggestion. In due course an invitation arrived for me to come to the sculptor's flat in Chelsea. I had a good dinner there, but as his plans for the rest of the evening became clear, I took my leave, accepting the refund for my fares on which he insisted. At home we had a good laugh about our naivety.

A more realistic proposal came my way. Learning that a kind of caretaker was wanted for a villa at Blenheim Road, Maida Vale, I grasped the chance with both hands. It meant a basement flat with separate entrance, one and a half rooms, with a scullery serving as kitchen, nothing to pay for rent, light and heating in return for some cleaning and keeping the coke boiler for the hot water going. A further attraction was that the larger room, formerly the kitchen of the villa, could also be used for group meetings. George Green mobilised his brother to paint the woodwork in bright colours. I shared the flat with Lola Reitz, who worked in the Vegetarian Restaurant until she went to Denmark to help Minna Specht in her school. Lola paid me a small rent and looked after the boiler when I started travelling; after she had left, Amy used to come over to help out with that. There was not much more I needed to earn for my other needs. Food was cheap, especially on the nearby Kilburn High Road stalls. There were some snags nevertheless. Not so much the Australian concert singer on the top floor who practised virtually the whole day; one got used to her. But there was dampness, and there were fat black cockroaches which penetrated everywhere; however hard we tried, we could not get rid of them. I was glad to move out, away from the cockroaches, when the time came and I could afford to rent a flat, a nice basement flat at King Henry's Road in Hampstead, which I shared with two other refugees; alas it too proved damp. After that, no more basement flats for me! Next, at Ridinghouse Street, near Oxford Circus, it was attic rooms again, shared by five group members. The main inconvenience: to carry our bicycles up and down three flights of stairs and find room for them on the landing.

How often I walked from Maida Vale to Amy's place and back! It took no more than half an hour and was healthy exercise, but burdensome to carry heavy bags with the papers, to which we subscribed jointly, and documents on which we were working. Especially in the fog! I remember one night when I walked home late in the worst "peasoup" fog I had as yet experienced, firmly clutching the typewriter Amy and I then used in turn, and a man suddenly emerged from the fog saying: "Can I carry this for you?" Fear of being robbed of our most valuable possession gripped me. It seemed a miracle that I did not lose my direction in the thick fog, and that the stranger vanished as noiselessly as he had come, swallowed up by the fog. During the war, fogs became an even greater terror in the blackout when I often lost my way. Industry had to clean itself up after the war; thereafter peasoup fogs lived on only as part of the London saga.

There was an anti-fascist relief fund at Transport House, established by the Labour Party in the twenties to support Italian refugees from Mussolini's terror régime. I never went near William Gillies, the party's international secretary who was in charge of the fund. Nor did most other socialists from Germany whose need for help and advice was much greater than mine. For to him *all* Germans were Nazis and he treated them accordingly. In contrast, Jim Middleton, the party's general secretary, and his wife Lucy were true internationalists, understanding and generous from the beginning. So were many local sections of the party, trade unions, trades and labour councils, co-operative societies and educational organisations like the Workers' Educational Association and the National Council of Labour Colleges. I had many opportunities to experience this when I began my lecture tours. All over the country, including Scotland, Wales and Northern Ireland I stayed in the homes of members; in those days speakers were rarely put up in hotels. My adjustment to British conditions benefited by this, and I made many friends, with some of whom links have endured to the present day.

However, before I could venture out to address meetings I had to improve my English. This did not take long since I had a good basis, and I used German rarely, as I was associating mainly with English-speaking people, which helped. David Fryd, another early member of the group, taught me a great deal. He came up specially from Canterbury, and I read books on politics and history to him. With great patience, he corrected my pronunciation. David impressed me by his intellectual capacity, but even more by his determination, rare for an Englishman, to teach himself German (which he managed within a year) in order to study Nelson's works. David died young and never reached his full potential.

George Green, on the other hand, was typically English in this as in other respects; he refused to learn a word of German, even when he married a German-speaking girl. He loved to tell the story about a Frenchman, a German and an Englishman who discussed the merits of their respective tongues. "Of course", the Englishman said, "we come out on top. Just take one example: a boy—the French call him 'un garçon', the Germans 'ein Knabe', while we simply call him a boy, and that is what he is." However, George was always willing to correct grammar or amend style in my English drafts.

The help thus received soon enabled me to take on translations into English. Moreover, at an early stage I was accepted as a tutor for one-year WEA classes on international affairs, thanks to Elisabeth Monkhouse and her sympathetic understanding of my position.

The two members who played the major part in the development of the Socialist Vanguard Group were Edith Moore and Allan Flanders. They had been students at the *Walkemühle,* and for both of them this had been a very formative period. They had become convinced that the advance towards socialism depends on the ideas of ethical realism gaining ground; they had come to appreciate the Socratic method as a means of training the mind in independent thinking; they had experienced solidarity in a close community. They had seen how much even a small group can achieve by a determined joint effort. For Allan in particular, the most impressive example had been the launching of the daily anti-fascist paper *Der Funke,* without financial resources, by the few hundred socialists of the ISK. Their experience in Germany had strengthened in Allan and Edith the resolve to build up, with others, a similar group of dedicated reliable socialists in Britain.

When I arrived in October 1933 Allan had already moved to the north, and, after some time, Edith joined him at East Herrington near Sunderland. Their visits to London and mine to East Herrington were frequent enough for close contact and co-operation. In later years we lived together with others in a community flat or house, first in London, then Sheffield, later again London. Both were able to give leadership in whatever group they worked. They supplemented each other in the close partnership which developed between them. Their qualities lay in different spheres. Allan's intellectual power, his fearlessly and carefully probing mind and his creativeness were exceptional. As he grew to maturity this was fully recognised, especially when, after the war, he became the leading expert in Britain in his chosen field of industrial relations. Edith relied largely on her intuitive powers and deep emotions; by her forthrightness, her integrity and moral fervour she had a strong influence on those who worked with her. Between her and myself there were clashes of personality, which often made our relations difficult. But these difficulties were contained by the aspirations and the work we shared, and by Allan who was a fair yet firm conciliator. Edith lived only till 1950, married to Allan at Oxford in the last period of her life. My friendship with Allan had its ups and downs, but was close and constant throughout the forty years of our co-operation until his death in 1973, which affected me deeply. "A light went out in my life the day Allan Flanders died", I wrote in *Socialist Commentary.* With Annemarie, his second wife, I maintain close relations.

My first visit to Edith and Allan at East Herrington was not my first visit to the north of England, but I remember my impressions vividly. In the throes of the economic depression, this industrial region offered a depressing picture indeed. I was familiar with Germany's industrial areas in a crisis, but I had never seen coalminers riding home in buses as black and dusty as they had emerged from the coal face, home to their wives who had to scrub their backs in the kitchen tub. Pit baths were then few and far between. On the other hand, I was struck by the fact that British working people—in the north east as elsewhere—lived far more often in a cottage or house, rented or owned, which they had to themselves, with more living space for their families than was usual in Germany. Another fact impressed me: the milk bottles delivered to people's front doors, and left there sometimes for hours before they were taken in. This would have been impossible in Germany, too many would have been stolen.

It was early on a Sunday morning that I arrived at Sunderland on my first visit. Since I had changed my plan at the last moment there had been no time for a warning to reach me about the inconveniences of a Sunday morning arrival, especially in winter. There is nothing like learning from bitter experience! It was bitter to find myself at Sunderland with more than five hours to wait for the departure of the first bus to East Herrington. There was nowhere to go; even the station was closed after all passengers had alighted. Walking up and down the streets I had plenty of time to take in the signs of decline which, I found, were more marked than elsewhere. Shipbuilding, the main industry, had virtually come to a standstill. I did not consider looking for a taxi; expenditure of this kind was outside our range.

On most journeys between London and Sunderland, heavy bags had to be carried, just as between Amy's and my home in London. In addition to papers and heaps of literature for sale at meetings, there was also the old sewing machine which we used in turn in the two places. Once at a social evening the usual games were played (beloved by British, strange to most German adults). In one of the guessing games, everyone had to write down their idea of paradise, and when the answers were read out the authors had to be guessed. I remember putting down with feeling: "Travelling without luggage".

Soon after my arrival from Denmark, on Amy's advice, I joined a local women's co-operative guild, and attended its meetings regularly. Not only did this help me in becoming fluent in English; I also learned to understand the Cockney accent. Moreover, I was introduced to local women's activities which, I found, played a much more important part in public life in Britain than they had in Germany. I learned about problems as reflected at the local level, about methods and customs in the Labour movement (of which the co-operative movement was an integral part, again different from Germany). I soon got over my astonishment at meetings being held in church halls and starting with a hymn. This was a far cry from the bitter struggle against the Church we had fought as German socialists. It was strange to learn about a religious service traditionally preceding the annual conference of the Labour Party, with Labour leaders reading the lesson. Likewise I, the ardent anti-monarchist, became adjusted to the different significance of the monarchy in Britain. After a time I ceased to resent standing up when "God save the King" was played in the theatre and on innumerable other occasions. At first, I admit, I was tempted to remain sitting, but soon I realized that such a protest was meaningless.

Amy herself was active in the co-operative movement. She was indefatigably campaigning on behalf of the workers on the tea plantations in Ceylon owned by the British Co-operative Wholesale Society. These efforts, I believe, resulted in some improvements but recently I was struck by reports about labour conditions there still being very unsatisfactory. I was roped in to help in these activities. In my Berlin days I had taken part in anti-imperialist campaigns of a different kind. They had been purely political and progagandist, while the Ceylon campaign was directed towards the achievement of immediate benefits for the people concerned. It was inspired by an awareness of responsibilities beyond national frontiers incumbent not only on governments but on one's own movement and its members with their stake in the colonies. I began to see what was involved in being a socialist within an empire.

Amy and Edith were also active in the movement for Indian independence, and I became interested too. They admired Gandhi and had studied his writings. They had met him in 1931 when he was in London for negotiations with the British government. It had been a memorable occasion. Gandhi had invited them to join him on his early morning walk to discuss non-violent resistance. Since he stayed in the East End of London, they had to rise at 2 a.m., and walk there to be in time for the appointment.

Edith maintained close contacts with Indian independence leaders, many of whom visited London after the war. Especially the socialists among them would come to see her, and we arranged meetings for them at our community house. I remember Achyut Patwardhan, Rammanohar Lohia, Asoka Mehta, Nath Pai among them. I, so to speak, inherited these contacts from her and, on my visits to India in the sixties, met many friends who had been to our house. I also took over from her writing for

Janata, the Indian socialist weekly, reporting on post-war developments in Britain and on the European continent.

This chapter has dealt with the way in which I took roots in Britain. It has described some of those whose help in this process was essential. Most important was probably the fact that I became at once part of a closely integrated group linked with the one to which I had adhered in Germany, in addition to my feeling of belonging to the Labour movement in general. All this emphasized again the continuity of the ideas shaping my life, of which I had become so deeply conscious in the weeks with Minna Specht in Denmark. The spirit of international solidarity which I personally experienced when I went into exile was exceptionally alive in all members of the Socialist Vanguard Group. Although I cannot mention them all here, I should like to add one name, that of the late Joe Madin, from whom I learned much about the British workers and the trade unions, especially in my years at Sheffield. Joe was a self-educated working-class leader with great wisdom gained from experience, and with an integrity which won him respect beyond the ranks of the Sheffield Labour movement to which, as President of the Trades and Labour Council, he gave sound leadership for many years (he died in 1967).

In remembering Joe, I often think of one occasion when he came to our house in Sheffield. Joe had taken it into his head that we, especially I, the German intellectual, needed to be reminded of what life was really like. At one of our weekly reading evenings at Strelley Avenue, when we took it in turn to read a piece of our choice to the others, he read a passage from one of Jack London's books—I do not remember its title. I am sure that he was determined to give us a lesson in realism. The story was about a man about to die of thirst and exhaustion in the desert, dragging himself on and on, followed by a jackal waiting to pounce. It certainly was a realistic, indeed a cruel and hair-raising description. And there was Joe, watching with a wry smile to see whether we, I in particular, could take it.

X

A New Germany and Europe

In the thirties it was natural that I should concentrate on questions related to Germany. This was not at variance with my becoming integrated into British society, nor incompatible with the steady widening of my international horizon. The German situation was of vital interest to Britain and the world beyond Britain. The fact that I happened to come from Germany was not decisive in determining my attitude, but it gave me a useful background of knowledge and experience.

Whenever I was asked to speak on Germany I accepted the invitation. The need to enlighten people on developments under Hitler and on the threat he represented internationally was constantly confirmed. Questions I had to answer again and again betrayed much ignorance. For example, the fact that Hitler had struck at his political opponents before touching the Jews was widely unknown. "But you are not Jewish", people would say to me, "so why did you have to leave Germany?" Another question was: "Is not Hitler doing something for Germany after all by giving people jobs and national unity?" A frequent comment was: "The Versailles Treaty was unjust. Now that it is a dead letter thanks to Hitler, things will surely quieten down". The influence of pacifist ideas in the Labour movement, as represented by George Lansbury, was still strong. Many left-wingers, anxious to avoid the question of British rearmament, and remembering Marx's words "proletarians of the world unite!", clung to the illusion that joining hands with the workers in Germany was the solution.

One day I read in the press that George Lansbury, just back from his visit to Hitler and impressed by it, would address a meeting somewhere in the East End of London. I felt that he should not go unchallenged, and went there. The meeting was packed by his admirers, many of them members of Labour women's sections, whom Lansbury assured that Hitler really wanted peace. No discussion was allowed, but by then I knew how to phrase pointed questions and managed to get in three. I was not popular, and felt lonely. But after the meeting, several people approached

86

me to express doubts about Lansbury's assurances, or even approval of what I had said.

In addition to lecturing I took up some journalistic work. I used the pseudonym of M. Jensen until I became a British citizen and no longer needed to take such precautions. Many of my articles were on Germany, but later also dealt with other subjects; they appeared mainly in the Socialist Vanguard Group's journal. I wrote, and contributed to, a few pamphlets, too. I also translated, for a fee, the *Deutschlandberichte*, reports on conditions in Germany issued in English (and French) after 1936 by the SPD in exile.

Practical things had to be done to support those who were fighting Hitler inside Germany. On these matters I worked in close co-operation with the German ISK members in Paris. Illegal workers who were in acute danger had to be helped to escape and find refuge somewhere. As the French government became increasingly hostile to socialist refugees—this was the case even under the Popular Front government led by Léon Blum, because of communist influence—the number of those for whom Britain was the only haven increased steadily. To secure entry permits British sponsors had to be found who were prepared to give legally binding financial pledges. I, and others, had to convince the sponsors that they would never in fact be held to these pledges. This was not easy, but there were enough who had the spirit and confidence to commit themselves in this way. It was encouraging to find such friends in this difficult period.

In 1940, when Minna Specht's school lost its teachers by the internment of German refugees—*all* then treated as "undesirable aliens"—places had to be found for the children.

The obligation I felt to honour the principle of solidarity was all the stronger since I had myself emigrated at an early date and never had to face persecution like others who had stayed behind. I escaped internment in 1940 during the panic caused by the German invasion threat. However, with Britain facing the real possibility of invasion, personal danger came closer to me, too. The attitude of British friends often amazed me. I happened to be in the home of a Durham miner, Bob McBeth, a member of our group, on the day when Churchill made his famous broadcast to the nation on the invasion threat. I could see on Bob's face that he refused to believe it would ever come to that. When I asked my friend Cynthia Rowland in Sheffield to explain to me the reasons for such an unrealistic confidence, she replied: "Of course, you would not understand. It is because of our history, because we were never defeated, never invaded for many centuries." Yet it was an active kind of confidence. Cynthia, for example, left her well-paid management position in a store in Sheffield to start working in a munitions factory in London to help the war effort.

In my realistic or, as some of my British friends thought, pessimistic mood, I made preparations for "going underground", and I was resolved to end my life if it came to the worst rather than fall into the hands of the Nazis. One day soon after the war, when I discovered in a drawer the deadly poison, I decided it was time to get rid of it. I walked to a canal in Maida Vale, and threw the jar into the water. It was a moment of lonely but intense rejoicing.

At the time, in that crucial year of 1940, I lived in Sheffield in a house at Strelley Avenue shared by four of our group. I had moved there at the beginning of the war with Edith, Allan and Charlie Buckner. The two men were working in industry as draughtsmen. Although I was not interned as an undesirable alien, the panic affected me all the same. The anonymous letters I kept receiving were probably inspired by neighbours seized by that panic. I went to police headquarters to complain, and perhaps this helped in stopping the letters. One significant incident of that period stands out in my memory.

One Sunday, after attending an open-air First-of-May rally, we returned home in the evening to find our house door broken in and the rooms ransacked. A number of blueprints were missing from drawers. We had not noticed that one electric bulb was not switched off when we left, so when darkness fell it had glared on to the street and attracted the police watching for offences against blackout regulations. We guessed they had been glad for a pretext to have a good look round our house. The blueprints they had confiscated were pieces of work Allan and Charlie had taken home from their firms to finish over the weekend. On Monday morning, Allan promptly went to police headquarters to complain about this arbitrary police action which "had held up essential war work". They humbly apologised and returned the drawings.

We found out what the local policemen, with their limited grasp of things, had reported as highly suspicious, apart from those blueprints: there were divans, instead of beds, in all the upstairs rooms, and typewriters everywhere! Undoubtedly I was the main cause of suspicions.

As the outlook for Britain and her allies in the war improved, the panic subsided. All our German friends were cleared by the Home Office tribunals. Those sent to the Isle of Man, Australia and Canada returned to London from internment. Other European refugees, among them many socialists, arrived in Britain from Nazi-occupied lands. There seemed then greater scope in London again for the work I was able to do, especially in the field of international relations. Political life in war-time Sheffield, as in other provincial towns, was rather subdued. Even the Federal Union movement which, with a fresh impetus, tried to promote new ideas for a post-war world in which national sovereignty would be overcome, had limited scope. So I returned to London in 1941.

In the years that followed, until the end of the war, I was closer than before to the circles of German refugees who were actively preparing the foundations for a united social democratic party and for post-war policies of reconstruction. I lived together with both British and German friends—about ten altogether—in an evacuated house at Alvanley Gardens, West Hampstead, which Cynthia and I jointly rented for "the duration of the war". How to furnish this large house? This was a problem, especially since our Sheffield house was still being maintained. By a lucky chance a solution was found. Two German families among our acquaintances had to store their furniture, also "for the duration". They were willing to let us use it, thus saving the considerable storage costs. There was a small snag: most drawers, cupboards and shelves were full of their things, leaving little room for ours. I dreaded the moment when this colossal mixture of belongings would have to be sorted out, in spite of the care taken in drawing up inventory lists. However, in the end, with good will on all sides, everything went smoothly.

Our house at Alvanley Gardens was a busy place. It served as centre for Socialist Vanguard Group work in which I was mainly involved. It was also a meeting place for German socialists including politicians like Erich Ollenhauer and Rosenberg as well as my old friend, Willi Eichler, who was then working for the BBC doing broadcasts to the people inside Hitler-Germany (they were listened to and encouraged many of our friends there, as they told us after the war). Minna Specht, who was a member of our household, was in contact with other German educationists and working in conjunction with prominent British people on plans for educational reconstruction in Germany. Leading Labour leaders from several continental European countries other than Germany, who had found refuge in London, came for discussions. They included André Philip, Henri Hauck and Jules Moch from France, Jef Rens and Paul Tofahrn from Belgium, Haakon Lie from Norway, Grosfeld and Drzewiecki of the Polish Socialist Party, Zygielbojm, Scherer and Blit from the International Jewish Bund, Luzatto of the Italian Socialist Party. They were all interested in co-operating with German as well as British comrades. The Socialist Vanguard Group was in a position to help in fostering these links. It arranged conferences and public meetings and issued publications to promote European co-operation. It fell to me to do a fair amount of the necessary work. For a time I edited *Europe Speaks* with reports from the Continent, especially on the resistance movements.

The Labour Party, as far as I know, showed no initiative in this direction until after the war when it took the first steps towards a revival of the Socialist International, a development into which I was soon to be drawn. But the Fabian Society's International Bureau organised meetings during the war in which many of the Europeans took part.

My links with German socialists remained close even after the war when new problems came to the fore and I had finally decided to stay in Britain. In the first place, the social democrats who set out to rebuild their movement in occupied and hungry post-war Germany under difficult conditions needed support, even to maintain their physical strength. We managed to send many food parcels, although rationing still continued in Britain. Having friends at the Vegetarian Restaurant, the Vega, was of great help then, as it had been in the preceding years.

Visits to renew personal contact in Germany had to wait till 1948 when entry restrictions imposed by the occupying powers except the Soviet Union were relaxed. I had been several times in France and Switzerland, for instance, before my first return visit to Germany. To cross the Channel once again was an exhilarating experience for me. I realised that I would always remain attached to continental Europe though Britain was home for me.

Meanwhile I did my bit for "German re-education" when this was started in Britain, by becoming one of the lecturers sent by the Foreign Office to German prisoner of war camps. By that time the recognised anti-Nazis had been released, the pro-Nazis and those of indistinct shades were left. It was strange for me to encounter these Germans after so many years of Nazi rule and war. The first time when I went to a camp, I was met by a prisoner of war at a small dark station in the country. When I drove with him alone in a jeep, I had an almost eerie feeling. I could not help thinking of how frightened I would have been in a similar situation in Germany years back when the same man was probably serving Hitler loyally.

This confrontation in the prisoner of war camps had a very limited value, while the courses at Wilton Park which started later, also under the auspices of the Foreign Office, were fruitful because the people who attended them and who were active in different spheres of life in Germany were ready to learn from meeting British people and to compare the institutions of the two countries. The POWs were not ready to absorb even the factual information put before them which had been withheld from them for so long. Desperate to go home, they were mainly interested in their rights as POWs under the Geneva Convention, an issue widely discussed in the British press. In my meetings I was often confronted with quotations from the *Manchester Guardian.* Some of the prisoners could read English and kept the others informed.

Since these camps were situated in rural areas where prisoners had to work in agriculture and since, as everywhere else in Britain, food and fuel were in short supply, their impressions of British life were miserable. I often challenged them when, over a cup of tea, their elected representatives made their invariably disparaging remarks about British backwardness. The most effective reply, I found, was the short question: "Is it not strange that Britain won the war?" They attempted no answer: perhaps some of them started thinking. Incidentally, no British officers were present on such occasions, nor during the lectures either.

I remember in particular one discussion about the question of German war guilt. I had not raised it; the question came from the audience. In my reply I spoke about the different degrees of German guilt, concerning not only the war but the crimes committed by the régime inside Germany and in the countries occupied by Hitler. Children could obviously not be blamed. The people who closed their eyes to the atrocities committed against Germans, other Europeans and especially Jews, could not be absolved from guilt, although their role had been a passive one. For Nazi activists, like dedicated stormtroopers, I could find no extenuating circumstances at all. When I said this, one could have heard a pin drop. Later I learned that this group consisted almost wholly of former stormtroopers. Yet the impression they had made when I had merely looked at the faces was of ordinary, rather simple-minded people, mostly the robust peasant type.

Since 1948 my visits to Germany have been frequent—for contact with relatives or old friends, more often to attend functions of the SPD or the Socialist International, or to give lectures. Thus I remained in close contact with developments in the Federal Republic of Germany. The SPD's international policy interested me particularly. I wrote a chapter on this subject for the English edition of *The History of the German Labour Movement* by Helga Grebing which I abridged for publication in Britain in 1969.

XI

Involvement in British Politics

My participation in British political life began at a relatively early stage. My connections with the British Labour movement, my close association with the Socialist Vanguard Group, my living together with British people, my good command of English, all eased my integration into British society.

Before long I felt at home in my adopted country. This was true of many German immigrants, even those who did not doubt that they would return one day to Germany. Since I did not want to live as an immigrant, I was acutely aware of the need to acquaint myself with the British outlook and background. By reading widely and utilising my contacts with British people, I tried to learn as much as possible. Certain things, however, were not easy to learn—the greater tolerance and flexibility, for instance, which I found in Britain. My approach had been shaped in a different climate. It reflected my German background, more particularly the influence of the ISK whose work, it is true, was affected by German conditions and needs though its attitude and methods were not necessarily typical of German ways.

The group I joined in Britain was prepared to accept, or try out, new things, even things foreign. Group members shared the belief that the validity of basic principles does not depend on the country of one's origin. Allan and Edith had brought back from the *Walkemühle* certain new ideas. They introduced, for example, the Socratic method of discussion. Yet some of my reactions and expectations must have seemed strange to my British comrades, and tensions developed at times. I vividly remember one occasion during a visit to Sheffield shortly before the outbreak of war. For a month I lived with several members of the Sheffield Branch in a tent in the Derbyshire hills near the city. Other members joined us for discussions in the evening or at weekends. Once a controversy arose over the selling of our journal. I insisted that all members should try to sell it not only among their acquaintances or at meetings or door-to-door but also in pubs, as we had done in Germany. Selling in pubs was intensely disliked by most. Moreover, many doubted the political value of this method. I remember pointing to the example of Tolle Fryd, one of the German friends working in the Vega Restaurant in London to help in earning money for the work of the ISK inside, and outside, Germany. Every month on Sundays, Tolle used to sell the record number of 500 to 600 copies of our journal in pubs and small shops in the East End of London, which she had discovered as a fertile ground.

Tolle—well yes, but could her example be followed? After all she was from Germany, used to unquestioning loyalty. Admittedly, her success was unique, her perseverance admirable, the financial result of her sales most welcome. But did she not succeed by her very personal approach which nobody could imitate? Because she knew little English as yet she relied on her smile and a few timid words. And what about the political significance of her achievement? Tolle herself thought that the journal would not be read, or read with profit, by most of those casual buyers in pubs. I had to admit that this was probably true. My arguments were, therefore, not wholly convincing. I also caused some resentment by expecting everyone to report on the results of their selling. If they failed to do so, I asked them point-blank. Some members felt that I behaved a little like an inspector general. Tensions of this kind often came into the open at a much later stage and in a subdued way.

The political situation in Britain struck me as similar in some respects to the one I had known in Germany. The United Kingdom, too, was engulfed by the economic crisis; only here it was not blamed on the Versailles Treaty! Unemployment, though not quite as high as in Germany, was disastrous and the British Labour movement had no more effective economic programme than the German movement. There were Fascists to be found in Britain, too. Oswald Mosley and his black-shirted gangs had just started making their appearance on the scene. I once attended a mass meeting at the Albert Hall where I witnessed Mosley's entrance, staged in true Hitler style. I felt almost sick. Still I was realistic enough to see that there was no danger in Britain of Fascist forces gaining the upper hand. Britain was not altogether free from danger in this respect, but the threat came from outside, not from inside the country.

The reactions to Hitler which I observed in Britain fatally resembled those in Germany when he began his ascent to power. The frantic preparations for conquering Europe, which started immediately after the conquest of the German people, were taken far too lightly. That national survival might be at stake was not recognised at that stage, and there was no will to act unitedly. Pacifist feelings and arguments still persisted among many British socialists, even for a period among my close friends. I found it difficult to have patience with these arguments. The emotional resistance to British rearmament was understandable, but it sustained the policy of appeasement towards Hitler. In agony we watched Hitler violating the clauses of the Versailles Treaty without meeting any opposition, and gaining more and more confidence in his pursuit of German rearmament, designed to enable Germany to launch a war. Clearly, the aim was a Europe organised on Fascist lines. How I disliked the *New Statesman* for sitting on the fence on this issue! Yet undeniably appeasement was widely accepted. All the more amazing the experience of 1940 when, with few exceptions, the British people responded whole-heartedly to Churchill's call for resistance.

It was agonising, too, to watch events in the Spanish Civil War (1936–1939). Many members of the Labour movement were deeply stirred by these events as their sympathies were strongly on the side of the Republic in its life and death struggle against Franco. Yet the Labour Party was not prepared to support the Spanish Republic's urgent call for arms. As in France with a Popular Front government led by the socialist Léon Blum, fears of international complications prevailed over sympathies with the Republic. For Franco was receiving help from Hitler and Mussolini. He also had the Catholic Church as his ally. This made us in the Socialist Vanguard Group all the more determined to support the Rationalist movement and, for a time, CIVIC, the Council for the Investigation of Vatican Influence and Censorship. I remember CIVIC's dynamic leader, the Irish Captain White, conferring eagerly with Allan.

On a visit to Liverpool, I was deeply shocked to discover in working-class areas bookshops and newsagents with lavish displays of pro-Franco propaganda in their shop windows. Catholic influence dominated wide sections of the Labour movement, especially the Irish. No sympathy in these sections for the International Brigade!

The Spanish war demonstrated the growing threat of Fascist forces in Europe and the weakness of France and Britain in meeting this threat. It also revealed the double-edged policies towards Spain of Soviet Russia and the Comintern (Communist International). It required courage to publicise the facts, especially on Soviet policy, when the Soviet Union supplied arms to the Republic and the Western powers supplied none. Since the Labour Party gave no leadership, unofficial action committees sprang up all over the country, campaigning for the Republic. Especially on international issues, such action was widespread in the thirties, but growing dissatisfaction over domestic problems such as mass unemployment and reductions in social benefits led to it too—the famous hunger marches, for example.

We in the Socialist Vanguard Group were highly critical of the Labour Party's ineffectiveness and lack of radical policies. Thus we participated in several of these action committees, some of them long since forgotten, as for example the First of May Committee of which George Green was the devoted secretary. Its aim was to induce the Labour movement to celebrate the First of May on the proper day as was done on the Continent, instead of the subsequent Sunday, in family outing fashion. In our journal we quoted Tawney who deplored "the void in the mind of the Labour Party" and "its lack of will for a new order". Tawney saw no hope for a change "till interests are hammered by principles into serviceable tools". Our group believed that it could help in the clarification of principles, and that under pressure from left-wing groups the necessary action might be brought about.

The disruptive tactics of the communists in trying to control any joint venture (they had thus disrupted the International Brigade even before the Spanish Republic's military defeat) underminded mutual confidence essential to co-operation. Personally I had lived through enough of this in Germany, but for some British friends it was a new and eye-opening experience. With the outbreak of war in 1939, "united front" affairs such as had flourished in the thirties came to an end. At any rate our group was no longer prepared to participate. The war situation ruled out strategies directed in fact, if not in words, against the Labour Party. But what changed our attitude was a more fundamental consideration. We abandoned the idea we had upheld, probably influenced by the example of the ISK in Germany as well as British conditions, that a group like ours was able to play an effective independent political role. We accepted the Labour Party realistically as the given political framework within which "peace aims" could be pursued and the tasks of reconstruction at home tackled. Allan Flanders, for instance, was happy to join the staff of the TUC to help in working out the trade unions' post-war programme and, after 1945, to accept the invitation of John Hynd as Minister for German Affairs to become political adviser to the British Control Commission in Berlin.

When the Beveridge Plan for social security was issued, we were clearly in favour, while some left-wing circles were still in doubt whether it would be advisable to "bolster up capitalism" in this way. We were delighted when we learned that Joan Robinson, the left-wing Cambridge economist, had made a pro-Beveridge statement. Social security and full employment, besides the nationalisation of key industries, seemed to us a sound foundation of Labour's post-war programme.

Though abandoning previous claims to independent political action, the

Socialist Vanguard Group maintained its educational activities and its own journal. Our summer schools, which continued throughout the war when the Labour Party had no such activities, were highlights. They were stimulating and clarified fundamental ideas as well as political issues of the day. They also offered cultural enjoyment and a memorable experience in community spirit. For several years after the war we kept on with these schools, to which we then invited friends from Germany, the USA, France, Switzerland and Italy.

My own active role in the Labour Party started in 1941, after my return to London from Sheffield. The Hampstead local party I joined had just gone through a considerable ordeal, having been undermined by a communist cell. It was in the process of being reorganised. All members were required to have two sponsors, and admission was by decision of the newly established executive committee. Unlike many other local parties which, in the absence of elections during the war, had more or less gone to sleep, the one at Hampstead was very much alive, with regular meetings and interesting discussions. Bombs, which frequently fell in the neighbourhood, did not prevent us from meeting.

Our able and fair chairman was Tony Greenwood. I admired even more our secretary, Florence Cayford. The way in which she tackled her organisational duties made me often feel very humble. After returning from a meeting, she would sit up for another hour or two to write the minutes. "I might be too busy next day", she said simply. For she was a busy housewife, mother and active worker in her local community. Later she became a local councillor, then a member of the London County Council, over whose Welfare Committee she presided for many years. In 1968–1969 she was Mayor of Camden. It was touching to see how the people of Kilburn, the solid working-class area where she has always resided, used to show their respect and consideration for their "Queen of Hampstead". They would refrain from holding her up when, formally dressed, she was hurrying to an official function. But when they saw her in her ordinary clothes, just out shopping, they would stop to talk about their problems. When in 1962 I moved from Willesden Green to Kilburn, I was happy to renew links with her and others with whom I shared memories of Labour Party work in the war years.

In 1945 I took an active part in the general election, the first held for ten years. This was a happy and exciting period for me. The nightmares of Hitler and the war were over. An era of peace was beginning which seemed to hold out prospects of progress. The Hampstead St Marylebone Fabian Society asked me to assume responsibility for a campaign among the new voters (the under-thirties) in the tradionally conservative Hampstead constituency. The "New Voters' Group" which we then formed included several members later to become well known in London county politics, for instance Bee Serota and Lyndal Evans. The aim was not only to reach new voters, but to train young Fabians in political techniques. Our campaign was keen and, as I vividly remember, imaginative. Vera Adamson, who was then the secretary of the local Fabian Society, wrote to me recently in remembering those days: "You did a wonderful job." In 1945 Hampstead was very nearly won for Labour; it was actually won once, in 1966.

Soon after the war, I was once the constituency's delegate to the party's Annual Conference. This sign of confidence meant a great deal to me, the former German. Actually Rene had stolen a march on me by being elected as a delegate to the Annual Conference in 1945 from the St Albans constituency. One of the youngest delegates present, she was proud to move her party's resolution and happy to dance at the Mayor's reception with Herbert Morrison. I did not have the chance to move the Hampstead resolution, which did not reach the agenda. But I had the satisfaction of seeing most of its proposals for the Labour Party's own international activities subsequently carried out. I did succeed in speaking in the debate on international affairs, and remember Ernest Bevin looking at me from the platform with evident surprise when I criticised some aspects of his foreign policy.

My attendance at nearly all the post-war Labour Party Conferences was useful for my lecturing and journalistic work. I never held party positions at any level—except lecturing at party summer schools or other functions. After 1950, I could not have done so anyhow because of my increasing international commitments. But I have always shared in local party work as much as I could. Only recently did I give up canvassing and other strenuous activities.

After my return to London from Sheffield, I became editor of *Socialist Commentary (SC)*. For a period during the war we were reduced to a duplicated edition because of paper shortage (the duplicating was done at our community house at Sheffield). In 1941, a return to normal became possible, and since 1942 *SC* has been published in London.

The editorial responsibility at first somewhat overawed me. I was worried about filling all the pages and drafting editorials in the light of the discussions at our editorial committee. For writing did not come easily to me. Many times I sat up all night struggling with an article. Willi Eichler, a frequent visitor to our house at Alvanley Gardens and himself an experienced former editor, often cheered me up. "Have you ever come out with blank pages?" he would ask me, "or without an editorial article?"

Looking at previous issues gave me courage.

I enjoyed the editorial work, and did it for fourteen years. The journal's purpose was close to my heart: to relate socialist politics to ethical values, and to analyse trends and events free from dogmatic pre-conceptions. *SC* at an early stage made a clear distinction between ends and means and thereby countered widespread confusion in socialist thinking, for example on nationalisation.

It often made me furious to see *SC* referred to as "right-wing". This happened especially when Hugh Gaitskell was treasurer of the journal's supporting organisation "Friends of *SC*". When "right-wing" means not to rely on nationalisation as the main means of socialist advance and to refuse to defend the Soviet Union's policies on the ground that the country is "socialist" and not "capitalist", it is not an objectionable term. But the idea of a weak-kneed opportunism and lack of far-reaching proposals are usually associated with it, arousing at once an emotional resistance among many Labour people. I believe that *SC*'s record over the years gives the lie to the implied accusation.

It was a tremendous gain for *SC* when Rita Hinden became associated with it. For several years we were joint editors. The first invitation to an editorial meeting, sent out by us jointly, caused a good laugh: the typist spelt our names as Mary Satan and Riot Hinden! In 1955, when I took over additional duties at the Socialist International, whose staff I had joined in 1950, Rita assumed sole editorial responsibility. She brought to it an outstanding gift as a writer and a great ability to extract the best from the contributors. She took endless trouble over improving presentation where necessary. Until her regrettably early death in 1971, her main concern remained with the journal. Her role in securing for it the important and acknowledged place in the movement was decisive and in this her close co-operation with Allan Flanders, chairman of the editorial committee, was a vital factor.

The renown and achievement Rita attained as editor was far greater than my own. Did this upset me? At times I felt some resentment, which is only human. But we both did our best in our different ways and in different circumstances. Rita always acknowledged that the foundations, not least the financial ones, had been laid by me and others working hard for many years. Her characteristic warmth and frankness spoke from a letter she wrote to me on 23 October 1955: "I have so much appreciated your willing partnership and all I have learned from you. The moments of difficulty we have had arise in any partnership, and they have been remarkably few compared with all the times we have worked very harmoniously together. What now falls on me in regard to *SC* is a heritage

Plates 23-26. International Activities.

Plate 23. Mascha Oettli, Mary Sutherland and Mary at an ICSDW summer school.

Plate 24. Rita de Bruyn Ouboter, Mary and Rosel Jochmann at the Seventh Congress of the Socialist International, 1961.

Fotografica EUR, Rome

Plate 21. Mary with Rene in 1973.

Plate 22. Mary in 1974 with Jean Brownlee.

Plate 19. Mary with Paul (1962).

Plate 20. Rene, Paul and Jonn (1976).

Plate 16. Allan Flanders.

Plate 17. Willi Eichler.

Plate 18. Mary in conversation with Willi and Allan.

Plate 25, Mary with Shubhangi—one of her daughters.

Plate 26. At a Mount Carmel Seminar—Mina Ben Zvi is on the left.

Photo-Emka, Jerusalem

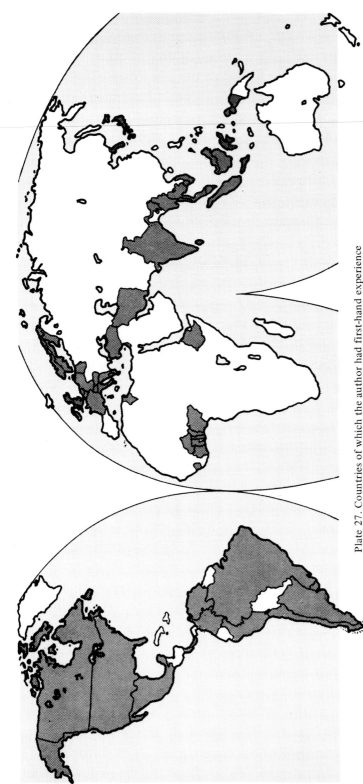

Plate 27. Countries of which the author had first-hand experience

Africa: Dahomey, Ethiopia, Ghana, Ivory Coast, Nigeria, Sierra Leone, Togo, Tunisia, Upper Volta

Asia: Burma, India, Indonesia, Iran, Japan, Malaysia, Singapore, South Korea, South Vietnam, Sri Lanka, Thailand

Europe: Austria, Belgium, Denmark, Eire, Finland, France, Germany (East and West), Great Britain, Greece, Italy, Luxembourg, Netherlands, Northern Ireland, Norway, Poland, Sweden, Switzerland, Yugoslavia

Latin America: Argentina, Brazil, Chile, Colombia,

*Costa Rica, Mexico, Peru, Uruguay, Venezuela

Middle East: Israel, Turkey

North America: Canada, USA

West Indies: Barbados, Guyana, Jamaica, Puerto Rico, Trinidad and Tobago of your work." Another letter which I cherished came from the late Frank Horrabin, the political geographer and cartoonist, who wrote on 29 October: "I feel that your resignation should not be allowed to pass quite so matter-of-factly. You were in charge in the uphill days, and the care, keenness and faith you put into *SC* has made later developments possible. I've never met anyone in the movement more regardless of limelight, but I do hope that you feel well satisfied . . ." I was glad to continue as a member of the editorial committee.

The Socialist Vanguard Group, to which *SC* owed its existence, came to an end a few years after the war. Its basis had proved too narrow for it to grow and be effective. Its members, together with a few dozen others, then established Socialist Union which set out to define anew, under the changed post-war conditions, the aims and principles of socialism. The need for such a reassessment was widely felt. Socialist Union, with Allan Flanders as chairman and Rita Hinden as secretary, responded to this need. Allan and Rita drafted the major publications which Socialist Union has to its credit: *Socialism, a New Statement of Principles* (1952) and *Twentieth Century Socialism* (1956). Both had a wide circulation in Britain and elsewhere. The preparatory discussions were a collective effort by the members. When it had accomplished what it had set out to do, Socialist Union was dissolved. We were confident that *SC,* with occasional special supplements produced by working groups, would continue to apply the same basic ideas to issues and problems of concern to the movement.

XII

Life in a Community and in the Family

For a considerable part of my life—nearly thirty-six years—I lived, with short interruptions, in a community. A start was made in Berlin in 1926 after the final break-up of my marriage, with six of us, all ISK members, renting a flat in the rather fashionable Hansa district; Renate joined us a little later, sharing my room with me. However, as a group of socialists we felt out of place in this typical middle-class neighbourhood. So we moved to the Wedding, a working-class area whose atmosphere has been described in a previous chapter. In Britain, as mentioned on other pages of these memoirs, I participated in various households, the longest and last period being from 1945 to 1962. We bought a large house at Dartmouth Road, Willesden, cheaply with the help of a mortgage and a loan from the group. It was not inhabited by the same people all the time, but most of us lived there for many, if not all, of the seventeen years. Because this was the one of our common homes that lasted longest I shall mainly refer to it in describing some features of our community life. But many features could be found in all common households shared by members of our movement. There were several—in Germany, France and Britain—which I knew only from visits.

There never was any general decision in the movement in favour of community living. The practice spread as the natural result of ideas, circumstances and practical needs. It offered a good framework for education, joint efforts and team work in the service of our aims, for the fellowship and solidarity in which we believed. The individual could be strengthened without the loss of independence which is so often connected with living in the usual family group. Vegetarianism—for us not a health question but one of making a stand against the exploitation of animals—was an added reason; an adequate vegetarian diet could more easily be secured in a common household. Political pressures, especially of the kind experienced in pre-Hitler Germany, emphasised the need for close links between like-minded people. Mutual understanding and support in such a community meant all the more when times were troubled and dangerous.

There were other practical advantages such as the saving of expenses and the enjoyment of facilities which most of us could not have afforded individually, including possibilities of entertaining others, a meal ready when coming home from work. For me, while Rene was a child, the problem of leaving her alone in the evening hardly ever arose, because someone was usually around. When we all wanted to go out together in Berlin to visit friends we would take her with us, and she would go to sleep there.

Our community homes at the same time always served as centres for group activities. They provided meeting places for functions not only of our own group but often of other organisations, for instance local Labour parties. Sometimes we had up to fifty people gathered at Dartmouth Road. For many years editorial meetings of *Socialist Commentary* were held there. Editorial board members from outside London like the Oxford economist, David Worswick, and the West Indian economist, Arthur Lewis, then in Manchester, could be our guests overnight.

Of the total of twenty-three living at Dartmouth Road over the seventeen years, most were members of the Socialist Vanguard Group and later of Socialist Union, one a member of the former ISK, one (her son) a former pupil at Minna Specht's school. Six were paying guests of the community, most of whom were with us for a period of months rather than years. A young girl came for a year from Germany to help Lola Reitz, our housemother. Lola had had the same function—an essential one in any community house—for a time at Sheffield and also at Welwyn Garden City. As for nationality, three were Indians, two Germans and one an Israeli; the rest were British, five of them with a continental European background. At the beginning we numbered nine residents, at the end seven. Members who left the community house wanted in most cases to build up a home of their own, being or getting married. Among most of us a relationship has continued to the present day which resembles that which members of a family usually maintain; for some of us it may even be a closer one.

At Dartmouth Road, international guests were frequent and they covered an ever widening range of countries. In the years after 1945, with the Labour Government as an interesting novelty, socialists and others from many parts of the world were especially attracted to Britain. Many found in our community house a welcome centre for meeting people informally. For a time, the Labour Party's International Department, then with Denis Healey as secretary, used to ask us to arrange informal meetings for some of its visitors from abroad. Over the years we developed techniques for dealing with the organisational work required for such occasions. Guests sometimes wondered at how much we seemed to take in our stride. This, at any rate, was what Jack, an American Negro friend of Allan Flanders, thought. His was a typical case.

Allan had met Jack on a visit to the USA and become friendly with him; he had assured Jack that should he ever come to London, there would be a bed for him at Dartmouth Road. One evening, when about thirty guests were already assembled, including several Africans, the bell rang and there was Jack, just arrived from the USA. The young girl who happened to open the door gave him no time to say anything except to murmur Allan's name. She ushered him in, he was warmly welcomed and drawn into a conversation. Allan recognised him as some one he had met before, but, on the spur of the moment, could not remember where. After a while, Jack managed to get a word in and said with embarrassment: "My taxi with the luggage is waiting outside." We then discovered that the telegram he had sent had not reached us, so we had not expected him. He was just thought to be one of Rene's African friends. Happily he stayed for a week or more before going on to Sweden.

Gatherings at Dartmouth Road were not always devoted to lectures and political talk or discussions. In the new year season we usually invited a large number of friends for a social occasion with fun and games, and sometimes a play performed by members of our community. In thinking back to these events, I often remember people who later became prominent in public life joining more or less gracefully in charades, "orange necking", guessing or other games.

The lighter side of our activities was inspired by those with a typically British frame of mind; I cannot imagine, say, a group of people in Germany indulging in the same kind of games—not a politically minded one anyhow. The sense of humour of British people, their refusal to take themselves too seriously, gradually left a mark also on our non-British, or naturalised British friends. It was reflected in the minutes we kept of our house meetings, composed for a time in rhymes which amused everyone when they were read out.

The basis for meeting our living expenses was simple. We shared them equally as far as things used in common were concerned; other expenses were the individual's affair. When special expenditure was envisaged, say for a stove in our terribly cold hall or a new stair carpet, this was discussed at a house meeting. Those who were earning more would pay most, or all, of it. For visitors, except those of interest to everyone, the one responsible for them paid for what they cost us. At times, some members helped others to retain their room during a period of studies elsewhere.

Our housemother was paid by the community. We all gave a hand in some of the domestic tasks. I loved my duty of cutting the hedges. On Sundays we took it in turn to cook the dinner; some of the male inhabitants started from scratch in acquiring this skill. Funny incidents invariably happened, as when Paul, after taking tremendous pains in making his first Yorkshire pudding, forgot to put it on the table and we discovered it shrivelled in the oven at the end of the meal. Claus, a trained electrician, spent a great deal of time on rewiring the house; we could hardly have afforded to have it done by an outsider.

Like any group of people attempting a common life, we faced problems. At times, they pressed hard upon us, but harder on some than others. Lola, who was responsible for the conditions of our daily life, and not always in good health, was most exposed to the demands from different members of the community—very different demands which might even be in conflict with each other. While the others had their life outside with its attractions and distractions, she was mostly at home, unable to escape from difficulties and tensions when they arose, and with a strong sense of responsibility towards everybody and towards the aims we were pursuing. Irritation was often caused by apparently small matters, by different habits we all brought with us from our varying backgrounds: tins left not properly closed so that the biscuits did not keep crisp; washing put dripping wet on the clothes line in the kitchen where everybody had to pass, to mention but two examples. Not surprisingly, noise, too, was the cause of some trouble, especially in the days when the house was overcrowded, and the over-sensitive thought the others were inconsiderate. Matters like these are part and parcel of a life together. What is important is the degree of adjustment and generous acceptance of differences of which everyone is capable. Our experience showed that some people are not able to fit into such a type of community life. For others the difficulties are too great to make the effort worthwhile. This is a fact to be accepted; good intentions do not alter it.

Nevertheless, I have found it rather amazing that we did find amicable solutions in most cases when problems arose and decisions had to be taken. The main reason, I believe, was that we shared convictions and purposes transcending the realm of narrower concerns in which problems and conflicts invariably arise. Moveover, most of us were deeply absorbed by professional and/or voluntary activities. Pressure of work and tensions were easier to bear since we were able to withdraw into our own rooms—more freely than is the case in most families. It is true, on the other hand, that this also meant loneliness for some at some time.

The ease with which questions of finance or belongings were settled seems to me remarkable. Whenever members moved out, and finally when we gave up the house, wishes and actual needs determined agreements reached. Members would take away with them things which they had brought in if they wished. The price we got for the sale of the house was divided equally among those with a share. Nora Henry, who had moved out not very long before the end, renounced her share for the benefit of the rest.

The Dartmouth Road community lost its original usefulness as a group centre, and some of its zeal, when the Socialist Vanguard Group was dissolved. It still remained valuable for those for whom it meant home and for the visitors who continued to be welcomed. For Rene and me, who introduced most of the international visitors, this value was outstanding, and we particularly appreciated the facilities available at the Dartmouth Road house, probably more than some of the others. For me personally, in all those years, the positive aspects of the community house outweighed the problems. At least in certain periods, the balance may have been different for some of the others. At the time, I was probably too little aware of this, being very much involved with my own work. This is what Lola tells me now, when we talk about old times.

Some members of the Dartmouth Road community were ready in 1962 to move out because they had reached the age when they preferred a smaller and quieter home. Rene and Paul were keen to start a home of their own for the first time. They asked me whether I would like to share it (which I did not take for granted) and I happily agreed, insisting however, that it should be on an experimental basis to start with. None of us has regretted the decision.

The flat we bought in 1962 in West Hampstead was large enough to enable us to pursue our individual interests and activities without necessarily involving or disturbing the others. At the same time, we have enjoyed the more intimate relationship which is possible in a smaller family community, and which we had not had an opportunity to develop before. Our flat has often served as a meeting place and the number of guests was probably as large as at Dartmouth Road. Many international visitors have found their way to 22 King's Gardens.

Soon we became four, instead of three, residents. In 1964, Jonn from Ghana, then thirteen years old, joined us. Gameli, as his parents called him, is the son of Rene's best African friend, and when he was born, Rene had written to his father: "Well, this is your fourth child, but I suppose you can have my share of children." Twelve years later, she thought that she should take a share in bringing up the next generation, and offered to give a home and education to one from the Adali-Mortty family, by then increased to five. Finally they sent their eldest son, mainly because he would one day carry responsibilities as head of the family, according to the custom of his country. But they assured us that the matter had been fully discussed within the whole family, and all had agreed.

Jonn has now completed the education and professional training for which we invited him to come to Britain. We are confident that he will make his way in life wherever it may be; our hope is that he will return to Ghana. However, we were not spared the difficulties often connected with teenagers in a family. They were probably intensified by the fact that Jonn was transplanted into a different cultural climate at the age of puberty, but in my view the problems would have been basically the same had he stayed at home, because they were rooted in his personality. Not having known Jonn since his early childhood was a handicap for Rene and Paul, who were uncertain at first in dealing with him. Moreover they had no experience of bringing up children. For many years they suffered agonies, and even despair at times when they feared that they were not giving Jonn sufficient help in overcoming his isolation, which led to lack of contact with and consideration for others. They were worried by his inability to tackle most of his school studies seriously, and his tendency to live in a dream-world, despite early intellectual alertness. It was perhaps Jonn's artistic bent, expressed in writing poetry and doing pottery, together with his love of music, which helped him through those difficult years.

Jonn has grown into an attractive, mature young man. After completing his formal education, he found a job in the central office of a large hi-fi firm in London, for which he had worked as a salesman during the summer terms of his "sandwich" course in business administration. In April 1974, he moved out from our home to share a flat with a friend. We were happy about his wanting to be independent but 22 King's Gardens is still his home, and we have a good relationship. Adopting him (not in the legal sense) did not only add a member of the young generation to our family unit but also made us virtually part of the Adali-Mortty extended family in Africa. On my two visits to Ghana I met many of them, and some—including his father, mother and one sister—came to stay with us for shorter or longer periods.

So far Paul has been only mentioned briefly as Rene's husband. Paul Branton came into our life soon after the end of the war. Like Rene, only more so, he has been a "late developer". Born as the son of a Jewish tailor in Vienna, he too was destined to be a tailor—or so his parents thought. He learned the trade, and had the opportunity to work in Sweden for a year, seeing another country, learning another language. When the menace of Hitler came closer to Austria, Paul went to Palestine, which almost certainly saved his life. There he lived at first with an uncle. The atmosphere provided by his relatives in Haifa was not congenial. He began to dislike his trade as well. "In any case", he asked himself, "what is the good of being a tailor here where most people are not wearing suits but shorts and open shirts?" He struck out on his own, working at different places, in a kibbutz, then in an office run by the British mandatory power, learning Arabic and Hebrew, making his own contacts. These included some who were interested in Leonard Nelson's philosophy. In addition to opening new vistas to him, this was a step—though unknown to him then—towards his future in Britain.

When the Second World War came, Paul joined the British Navy. He spent six years in its service, in Haifa, Benghazi, Cairo and finally Rome, where he became fluent in Italian. His rank was that of a "leading writer", the equivalent of a corporal in the army. I had never heard this term before, and promptly read it as "leader writer". There were anxious moments when the German army came close to his unit in North Africa, for his papers showed that he was from Palestine, i.e. Jewish.

After the war was over, Paul had to decide where to go. Vienna, where his parents and other relatives had died, did not attract him. Nor did Palestine, since Paul was not a Zionist, and his memories of his years there were not happy. Through a friend connected with Minna Specht and with Nelson's ideas he obtained my address in London, and wrote to me. The earnestness and sincerity which spoke from his long letter impressed me, and I decided to help him to come to Britain. There were then only two possibilities: either as a coal miner or as an agricultural worker. David Thomas, a close friend and member of the Socialist Vanguard Group, agreed to do what he could. He obtained a work permit for Paul to work on his fruit and vegetable farm in Kent, which he did for two years. Because of his service in the Navy Paul was able to apply for British citizenship and was naturalised within six months of coming to Britain.

Then Paul became a member of our community at Dartmouth Road in London. He worked in the office of *Socialist Commentary* for nearly ten years while taking evening classes in philosophy, which was his favourite subject. This interest led him to the study of psychology. He was very happy when he was admitted to Reading University for a three-year degree course in psychology, and when the question of a grant was solved. Later, specialising on research in ergonomics, he worked for the Furniture Development Council, an innovation introduced by the Labour Government after the war, then for the Medical Research Council, finally for British Railways. His previous varied practical experiences were an asset in the career he finally chose which is concerned with the human factor in industry.

PART THREE

XIII

International Experiences

In 1919, soon after the end of the First World War, I had my first experience of a journey abroad. Chance circumstances led to my visiting Denmark. An aunt of mine had met a jovial Danish businessman at a trade fair at Leipzig, the first to be held there after the war. He was going around with cases full of the famous Danish *smörbröd* (open sandwiches) which he offered to Germans he befriended. He was probably attempting to clear his conscience, having made good profits by supplying war-time Germany with bicycles and other goods from neutral Denmark. He was also looking for a young German girl to invite to his home in Copenhagen as a companion for his wife who was grieving over the recent death of their elder daughter. My aunt suggested my name, and, in due course, an invitation from the Rammel family arrived.

With some difficulty I obtained a passport, a newly introduced requirement; in pre-1914 days passports had been unknown. Shortly after my arrival in Denmark, a little comedy of errors occurred. Unexpectedly, a second German girl appeared on the scene—another result of Mr Rammel's sandwich-supported contacts at Leipzig. Not long after that (they had been expected) two small Austrian boys arrived from starving Vienna where another business trip had taken Mr Rammel. The villa was not very large, but all were made welcome. The boys were sent to the German school, and eventually stayed for good. One of them became head of the prosperous business when Mr Rammel died, and the other one works there too.

Thus my earliest venture abroad was not linked to my work or my social and political interests as were most of my subsequent visits to other countries. But international relations were even then among my foremost concerns. Friendships formed in Denmark on that first occasion lasted for many years.

Before becoming conscious of being a socialist I was a convinced internationalist. This influenced the choice of the first political party I

111

joined. I preferred the USPD to the SPD mainly because it had opposed
the war credits and in my view had shown itself truly concerned with the
internationalist aspirations of socialism. However, I went into the SPD
when the minority of the USPD was reunited with it, after its majority had
merged into the Communist International (Comintern).

Why was I not drawn in that direction? The Comintern claimed to
be the true heir to the Labour movement's traditions of international
solidarity. Like many of my generation I had welcomed the Russian
Revolution. It aroused new hopes in contrast to the bitter disappointments
we suffered in Germany over the missed opportunities for radical social
change when the old régime broke down and power was there to be
grasped. We knew that revolutionary change meant a violent upheaval, and
we made allowances for the need of Soviet Russia to defend herself against
reactionaries from within and without. But soon we were asking ourselves
worrying questions. Would the terror in Russia be confined to reactionaries? Nelson had made very clear the dangers inherent in a collectivist
economic system with all power concentrated in the hands of the
government, the dangers of bureaucratic tyranny and mismanagement.
Would Lenin defy the collectivist dogma when faced with these experiences? Would he find a worthy successor?

Rosa Luxemburg had warned against another danger, that of the
centralist party destroying the revolutionary zeal to be found in the
soviets. She had seen early signs of this in Russia. I had heard her speak
shortly before she was murdered in January 1919 and was impressed by
her integrity, her courage and her humanity. These spoke from her letters
from prison, a book we eagerly read in socialist youth circles. Who could
then foresee the horrors of Stalinist rule? Evidence from Russia was slow
in coming through. Yet even at an early stage we witnessed in Germany
the effects of disastrous Comintern tactics: uprisings with no chance of
success, which only strengthened the reactionaries. The dark hours of
1940 were still a long way ahead when Soviet Russia would surrender to
Gestapo officials at the German frontier German communists who had
escaped to the Soviet Union from the Gestapo terror!

Many people, and not only party communists, shut their eyes to all this
because of their sympathy with the Russian Revolution and their fervent
belief that the common ownership of the means of production established
in Soviet Russia would guarantee a socialist society (I never shared that
belief because I never identified socialism with collectivism). But again and
again it happened at later stages that Soviet politics touched people on the
raw, and they had rude awakenings. Former communists from various
countries gave an account of this in the important book edited by Richard

Crossman, *The God that Failed*. I remember British Labour people who joined the International Brigade to fight against the fascist forces led by General Franco in Spain, full of admiration for Soviet Russia which—unlike Britain and France—had sent arms to the Republican side, but who returned bitterly disillusioned having witnessed the destruction of the Republic's most loyal socialist and anarchist supporters at the hands of Soviet agents. More recently there was the even more sobering experience of Soviet Russian intervention against Hungarian, then Czechoslovak workers who had attempted to "humanise" communism. Thus my own early and decisive experience in Germany was echoed throughout several decades.

It was in the democratic Labour movement that I began to participate in international co-operation. In 1923, the Labour and Socialist International, as successor to the Second International which had collapsed in 1914, came formally into existence. Parties as well as trade unions were associated with it. My first personal acquaintance with its activities, which was in the trade union field, dates back to 1924. It was a more humdrum experience than we in the socialist youth movement had imagined when joining in the refrain of the workers' song "the International fights for human rights". These words expressed the International's continuing purpose, but the preceding words "the last battle let us face" no longer corresponded to the more realistic mood born of the First World War and the failures and setbacks that followed. There was no "last battle" on the horizon, but a long succession of battles, campaigns, activities, efforts and sacrifices. The struggle would be on many issues and on many fronts, including the newly established League of Nations on which many socialists pinned some hope now that the belief in the workers preserving peace by combining their forces against the capitalists had been shattered, and there was no prospect of its resurrection. In the circumstances the first need seemed for reorientation.

This reorientation in the early twenties implied less reliance on revolutionary hopes and quick results, while paying more attention to practical tasks even though their realisation would perhaps take a long time. The fostering of better international understanding was one such task, and it demanded reducing the language barriers. The case for an international language generally adopted all over the world seemed compelling. Therefore, like other members of the ISK (which issued some publications in Esperanto) I learned Esperanto. When I attended an international congress of Esperantists I was very impressed. Internationalists, I believed, should support Esperanto and press for a decision, in particular by the newly established League of Nations, to introduce it as a second language in the schools of all countries. Alas, notwithstanding the good arguments for Esperanto it made no headway because of prejudice and lack of good will. Personally I became wholly absorbed by the political storms which finally landed me on the British shores and continued to keep me occupied there. But on one occasion in my early years of immigration I had a rather unusual reminder of the fact that I was an Esperantist.

The occasion arose during the Civil War in Spain through my contacts with British Esperantists. A German friend of mine, an anti-fascist refugee like myself, had participated in the war in Spain, but then moved to Paris. The Esperantist group in Manchester invited him to speak at various meetings about his experience in Spain. He was to speak in Esperanto—he knew no English at all. This, it was thought, would demonstrate the practical value of Esperanto before a represenative body of the Labour movement. Because of visa difficulties, the visit had to be cancelled, and I was asked to take my friend's place. Nazi Germany, I was assured, would be an interesting subject, too, but I would have to speak in Esperanto and pretend not to know any English. Otherwise the intended purpose would not be served. I allowed myself to be persuaded to accept. My Esperanto had become rusty, but Amy Moore, herself a keen Esperantist, helped me in drafting a speech and wrote down the main terms likely to be needed in discussion.

My first appearance was at the Manchester Trades and Labour Council. The meeting was packed, and all went according to plan. But I disliked the farce of pretending to know no English and refused to repeat it at other meetings, though I was willing to discuss in Esperanto with the Esperantists. Shortly afterwards, one of the trade union delegates I had met in Manchester happened to be present when I gave a lecture elsewhere. He was utterly amazed at my having learned perfect English in such a short time! How had I done it, he asked me. I replied that I was not in a position to solve this mystery for him.

Back to international relations in the twenties. Together with my friend Nora Block I attended an international trade union summer school in 1924, lasting two weeks and held at Ruskin College, Oxford. Opportunities for personal contact and exchanges of view represent the main value of most international gatherings provided there is freedom of discussion and a congenial atmosphere. From the Oxford school I remember particularly Julian Besteiro, a prominent Spanish socialist, one of those who found a tragic end in the final stages of the Spanish Civil War. The group of trade unionists to which Nora and I felt specially attracted was the one from the Irish Republic. We were fascinated by these fierce-looking Irishmen with their penetrating blue eyes as we listened to their accounts of the then still recent struggle for national independence. How revealing to see Britain for the first time through Irish eyes! Perhaps we were carried away a little by our personal sympathies, but we were disappointed when Nelson and other friends in Germany received our reports with scepticism. They challenged our apparent assumption of the progressive rôle of Irish nationalism, particularly in view of the power of the Catholic Church in that country. Still, I was stimulated to read about Irish history.

After the fortnight at Oxford Nora and I spent another two weeks in London attending functions of the ILP, in particular, and meeting many people. When an unexpected sum of money arrived from a friend of Nora's with the proviso that "we should enjoy ourselves", we decided to have a look at the Netherlands on our return journey. In the young Dutch trade unionist whom we had met at Oxford we had a wonderful guide. Three main impressions have remained with me from this first short exploration of the Dutch scene: visiting new workers' housing estates, evidence of Dutch pioneering in the sphere of housing; talking with diamond workers, self-educated loyal Labour supporters, at their place of work and at home with their families; walking one night through Amsterdam's harbour quarters with their appalling display of prostitutes.

In the following year I set off on my own on another European tour. This was in connection with my visit to Marseilles as the German delegate to an international conference of young socialists which was held on the eve of the Second Congress of the Labour and Socialist International. I remember little about either the youth conference or the congress to which I was admitted as a visitor. But I recall that I found some congress debates bewildering, in particular when several fraternal parties from the same country—three or four from Czechoslovakia—fought each other heatedly over policy questions. I realised how arduous and complex a task it is to promote understanding and unity not only among socialists of one and the same country but also of one and the same International. I had contact with some of the British delegates who seemed to mix very little with others. I felt uneasy about the fact that they all stayed at the most expensive hotel since the British workers were far from affluent in the twenties. But one of them told me, shrugging his shoulders, that for Britishers this was the natural thing to do.

Before Marseilles I spent a few days in enchanting Paris. Interesting, though not exactly enchanting, was the first glimpse I had there of a French Socialist Party Congress with its protracted sessions and never-ending speeches, but some admirable rhetoric too. From France I went to

Italy, where fascism had come to power under Mussolini. After the murder of its leader Matteotti in 1924 the Socialist Party had been prohibited; there was no possibility for me to contact socialists. Then on to Austria for my second visit to that country. Again I was struck by the amazing feats of organisation performed by the Austrian Socialist Party, always the most solidly organised of all the International's affiliates.

I was able to cover much ground with little money by travelling at night, which saved hotel expenses, and patronising cheap eating places (in Italy, I often shocked the waiter when ordering no further dishes after the first course of spaghetti which for me was an ample meal). Friendly people everywhere gave useful advice. I carried all my luggage in a rucksack, a habit continued from my German *Wandervogel* days, which in France however caused many stares. The fact that I, a young woman, was travelling on my own frequently caused more than stares! I was keen on seeing beautiful scenery and cultural treasures, but my main interest then and ever since was to learn about conditions, to talk with people and, in so far as this was practicable, share with them part of their lives, if only for a brief span.

On my first day in France, before proceeding to Paris, I visited the left-wing writer, Henri Barbusse, who became internationally known in the twenties for his courageous reports on the oppressive right-wing régimes in the Balkans. His book exposing the "white terror" appeared in 1926 with the title *Les Bourreaux* (The Hangmen). I have vivid memories of that day. After a night's journey I left the train at a small station, deposited my rucksack and walked for an hour, in the freshness of a beautiful summer morning, to the village where Barbusse lived. I appeared at his house rather too early for him—he was not up yet. Nelson, who had corresponded with Barbusse, had asked me to discuss certain matters with him; as far as I remember they concerned a German translation of his work. The hours passed like in a dream, for I fell in love with this Frenchman whom I had not seen before, with his broad sweep of ideas and beautiful language. He was so open to what life had to offer, but also so passionate in his concern for those who suffered injustice, a concern unimpaired by his own suffering (he was ill with tuberculosis). A few years later I saw Barbusse again in Berlin when there was the same immediate contact between us as had so deeply touched me on the first occasion. I treasure several of his books which he sent me when they came out.

My encounter with Barbusse in 1925, so I felt then in my enthusiastic mood, had been my personal introduction to the cosmopolitan spirit of the French Revolution which had produced the declaration on the rights of man and was alive in the best of France's intellectuals. That night in

Paris, I formulated in my mind the thesis that, in order to know another country, one has to be in love with someone belonging and attached to it. Putting the idea a little differently, I still believe that only by becoming involved, by entering into some closer relations, by friendships rather than mere acquaintanceships can one come nearer to understanding the people of another country.

There was no further international travel for me in the years which followed, except for some holidays spent in Switzerland, Italy and, with Renate, in Denmark. I was as keen as before on widening my international horizon, but as the internal situation in Germany worsened it absorbed me to an increasing extent. Moreover, from 1926 my professional obligations allowed me less freedom of movement. I used much of my free time, at weekends in particular, for travel within Germany to lecture and attend various political functions. Often I returned to Berlin on a Monday morning and went straight to work.

Throughout the era of the Weimar Republic, even in the years of economic crisis, Berlin was a very lively city, culturally and intellectually. It was the centre for many international events. Thus I had many opportunities for meeting people from all over the world. In the early twenties, for example, I had frequent contact with the circle of young politically interested Chinese around Madam Sun Yat Sen, widow of the founder of the Kuo Min Tang. I knew several of those who tended towards the Left and, on their return to China, perished in Chiang Kai-Tshek's persecutions of the communists.

The year 1933 took me to Denmark, then to Britain for good. From there, between 1933 and 1939, I visited Paris once or twice a year, mainly to keep in contact with German ISK members and with efforts to support resistance to Hitler inside Germany; my contacts with French socialists were limited at that time. In London I gradually became familiar with the problems of India, Ceylon and other parts of the British Empire.

The war years brought isolation from the European continent in a geographical sense, but close relations with refugees from many parts of Europe, including leading socialists. Meetings of the Socialist Vanguard Group attracted also a number of socialists and trade unionists from the USA, stationed in London with the US army. This resulted in some close contacts, which continued after the war.

Looking back on that whole period, I see it as an invaluable preparation for the work in the Socialist International which—I did not know it then—I was to start in 1950. My lecture tours and visits in the immediate post-war period to Switzerland, Germany, Italy and France gave me an insight into conditions generally, and in particular into developments in Labour and socialist organisations. While, in the thirties, I had spoken to British audiences about Hitler Germany and fascism, I was now in demand as someone who could talk from first-hand experience about the new Labour Britain, a subject which was then of tremendous interest. There was an amusing newspaper report on one of my meetings in Switzerland. The press reporter, drawing on his imagination rather than available information, described me as "a typical tall English lady", a Member of the House of Lords, who spoke German fluently with hardly a foreign accent.

When, as a British Labour Party representative, I attended the first summer school of the French Socialist Party soon after the war, I met there socialists from East European countries who had not yet been forced into the so-called united workers' parties promoted by the communists. Yet they no longer dared to speak their own mind in public, because they knew someone had been instructed to report on them. Privately, I heard moving stories from socialists about communist intimidations which began as soon as Nazi Germany's rule had come to an end. I remember a young Pole saying in his melancholy voice: "I survived the Nazi terror, but I doubt whether I shall survive this new oppression".

After the summer school, I stayed in France for another week together with Pearl Veerhault, a young English comrade. I was anxious to get to know the mood of post-war France. In London I had been reading with keen interest the paper *Combat,* especially the spirited editorials by Albert Camus. They had aroused great hopes, both inside and outside France, for a future France in which the influence of the anti-Nazi resistance movement would augur well for social and political progress. Previously, in Paris and Lyon, and during the summer school, I had met leading socialist representatives of the resistance. Now, in that second week in France in 1947, my contacts were at grass roots level.

Pearl and I found accommodation in a small village in the Loire region in the home of a slater who worked in the nearby town. He was a life-long socialist and introduced us to his local party, which was in the process of re-establishing itself. We were allowed to attend a special meeting where we witnessed a trial of former members accused of collaboration with the German occupying forces. The atmosphere was loaded with emotion, but the procedure was fair. In some cases re-admission to membership was decided, in others permanent exclusion. There could not have been a more telling and moving story of what French people had gone through under Nazi occupation.

Our host was sternly anti-German. So I thought it wise not to tell him about my origins. He was evidently unable, as yet, to distinguish rationally between different sorts of Germans. Friendly relations soon developed between us and our hosts. We shared our food (we had brought some rationed goods from London), cooking it on a tiny paraffin burner in the courtyard; to save money, the gas stove in the kitchen was used only in the winter. We accompanied "Madame" on her visits to nearby farms and on her tours of the village. Twice a day she went to feed her rabbits, housed about twenty-five minutes away from her home. Madame soon showed her desire to accompany us on our excursions in the neighbourhood. A clear indication of this desire was her squeezing her huge form into a corset with her bedroom door wide open so that we could not fail to notice. We went by coach, or sometimes in the car of a teacher we had met at the summer school. We were glad to invite Madame. The family refused to accept any money for our room, insisting that they owed the British a debt for defeating Hitler.

Madame was less rigid in her attitude to Germany than her husband. She told us frankly, but in strict confidence, about a German soldier who had helped the villagers where he could, and had recently revisited the village to renew contact. Her husband must not know that she had seen the man! "We women cannot help looking at people as human beings", she said.

In 1948, on a visit to Germany, I attended as a visitor the congress of the reconstituted SPD at Düsseldorf. One day, an emergency arose when Sam Watson, a British delegate to that congress, who was to address a conference of German miners' delegates at Dortmund, could not be found anywhere when the time came for him to leave the congress hall. Unaware of his commitment, he had gone to sample wine at a far away place by the Rhine. I was asked whether I could help out and speak on the situation in the nationalised coal industry in Britain, a subject not within my usual range. By a lucky chance I had with me in my briefcase a copy of the first report, just published, of the National Coal Board, which I had been studying. More luckily still, I also had with me extensive notes I had made of a lecture given by Sam Watson on the same subject a short time before at a Labour Party summer school which I had attended as a lecturer. The fact that I had been down a mine several times, both in Germany and Britain, might also be of some use, I thought. So I agreed to go. The interpreter booked to accompany Sam Watson got an evening off as I could make the speech in German. How amazed the miners were to hear a woman from Britain speak competently about such a male occupation as coal mining! And in perfectly good German! On the next evening I went with Sam Watson to a meeting in another mining area to interpret for him. Comparing his speech with my effort of the previous night I was reassured; apparently I had not done badly. At that second meeting there was an embarrassing moment in the discussion. One of the miners, after stating that he had been against the Nazis, added: "Of course, I did not want Germany to be defeated—we can see the bad results now!" What a difficult task, I thought, German re-education, so much talked about then, would be.

This was also the period when I extended my knowledge of Asia and Africa, not—as yet—by visits to these continents, but by meeting representatives in London who came to our house. I have referred to the Indians before. Our Burmese visitors included members of the first government who were returning from a conference they had attended in Geneva. Tragically nearly all, if not all, of them were assassinated in Rangoon not long afterwards in a vicious assault on the cabinet in session. This deprived newly independent Burma of highly qualified leaders whom it could ill afford to lose. I followed Indonesia's post-war struggle for freedom from Dutch colonial rule closely through a Dutch friend, Sal Tas, correspondent of the independent Dutch paper *Het Parool,* a friend of the socialist Sutan Sjahrir, the first Prime Minister in independent Indonesia, whose widow I was to meet many years later on a visit to Indonesia.

XIV

Working for the Socialist International

When in 1950 I was offered the chance of working for the Socialist International, I seized it eagerly. I was elated by the prospect of utilising my experiences, my linguistic, journalistic and editorial skills in the revival of an historic institution which embodied world-wide socialist developments over nearly a century. After years of freelance work, it also seemed good to work once again within an established framework. Actually it was not too firmly established yet when I joined the staff of COMISCO, the Committee for International Socialist Co-operation provisionally set up soon after the war to restore relations among Labour and Socialist parties. By 1950, it had at last acquired a small office of its own and a secretary, Julius Braunthal, and was setting about preparing the Frankfurt Congress of 1951. There the Socialist International was solemnly proclaimed as successor to the First, the Second and the Labour and Socialist International. The Congress adopted a declaration on "Aims and Tasks of Democratic Socialism", a statute and an organisational structure. I felt very much part of the new International, and found it stimulating to participate in an important post-war political development.

Not surprisingly, at a time when most European member parties had to build up from scratch, the resources of the International were pitifully small. From COMISCO's three tiny rooms behind Oxford Street we moved, after Frankfurt, to a small house in a side street in Knightsbridge. These premises were not impressive either, at any rate not according to the veteran Belgian leader, Camille Huysmans, a former Secretary of the Labour and Socialist International. He voiced his horror in no uncertain terms. After climbing the narrow stairs, he proclaimed that the International should have its headquarters *"dans les grands boulevards"*. He kept on repeating these words as if they provided a magic formula for more prosperous days. The rooms then taken in Euston Road in a house soon to be demolished, though in a main street, would certainly not have satisfied Huysmans either, nor would those still occupied today in St

121

John's Wood High Street, often referred to as "that place above the greengrocer's shop" by press correspondents who had probably stumbled over piles of vegetables when searching for the entrance door.

The Congress at Frankfurt impressed me as an encouraging demonstration of the recovered strength and confidence of Social Democracy, though I was too busy to fully enjoy the glory of the new start. The Congress reflected a new mood, as did the statement adopted by all except the Japanese Socialist Party which was still wedded to more traditional formulations. The International's approach which was democratic socialist rather than Marxist, marked an adjustment to new conditions in the post-war world.

Working behind the scene, I helped to cope with organisational problems. I was rapporteur, and the only one taking notes for days on end. That there was no simultaneous translation was in itself a drawback, but for me it was a blessing in disguise. For it gave me a breathing space between speeches and time to complete my notes. However, the same speech repeated in another language afterwards was not necessarily the same speech, at any rate not when the late Samuel Grumbach, a bi-lingual Alsatian with an irrepressible temperament, pushed the German translator aside to do his own German version—which usually turned out to be a very different oration.

Even before the start at Frankfurt, a problem concerning the English text of Kurt Schumacher's opening speech was handed to me. Schumacher's ideas were complex, his style was involved; the translator who had been engaged had simply given up and gone home. What happened to the French text I do not know, but I had to sit up half the night to complete the English version, helped by my friend, Susie Miller, who knew Schumacher well enough to explain to me what he meant.

Another incident which I remember happened at the very end of the Congress. A bundle of twenty stencils for the International's Information Service, which were to be duplicated early next morning and had still to be proof-read, vanished from my pigeon hole in the reception hall while I went to have a coffee. On my return, I discovered that everything had been cleared away; the staff had suddenly gone to join an evening excursion. I was in despair. A steward of the SPD who was clearing up the hall still remembered me from pre-Hitler days in Berlin. "I'll find them for you, Comrade Maria," he said reassuringly, "they must be in one of these cupboards." The cupboards were locked; the keys could not be found. My friend nevertheless kept his promise. Being a locksmith he knew how to force open a door. Clutching my precious stencils, I thought: long live old comradeship!

Conditions were often difficult for the few of us at the Secretariat, but we were happy because our hearts were in the work. My friendship with Inge Deutschkron, Braunthal's first energetic secretary (now living in Israel as a journalist), has endured to the present day. It was cemented among other things by the fun we had together over involuntary jokes caused by people's imperfect knowledge of languages not their own. We had a steadily growing collection with which we sometimes entertained friends who had a feeling for the funny side of things. One example of many: at a study week on party organisation and propaganda techniques, Nina Andersen from Denmark commented in the discussion on the floating vote, but called it the "loose votes" which corresponds to the Danish term *løse stemmer*. Many women, she pointed out, were among this group. "We must do something about the loose women's vote," she said excitedly. Why was there such hilarious laughter, she wondered. Was the women's part once again taken lightly? "Yes, comrades", she repeated with even greater emphasis, "we can lose or win an election by the loose women's vote!"

The happiest of all was undoubtedly the Secretary, Julius Braunthal, confirmed by election at Frankfurt. He had once served on the staff of the Labour and Socialist International. Now holding a position at one time occupied by his famous compatriot Friedrich Adler meant very much to him. I am sure he felt like an instrument of history chosen to resurrect the International after fascism and war had made havoc of its work and destroyed many of its leaders.

When the first issue of the International's *Socialist International Information (SII)* appeared on the first of January 1951, Braunthal with a beaming face helped for hours on end in packing the two thousand copies we dispatched. His deep emotional commitment to the International had a touching, childlike quality about it, as had the optimism born of his belief in the final victory of socialism. This may well have impressed particularly his friends in Asia, who also admired his knowledge of the movement's history of which, to them, he seemed a piece. They often referred to him as the grand old man of European socialism. Sometimes his sentiments led to somewhat strange actions. I remember one occasion in 1954 when, in honour of the ninetieth anniversary of the First International's foundation, a delegation laid a wreath on the grave of Karl Marx at Highgate Cemetery. Braunthal later asked a member of the staff to retrieve the wreath in the dark of the next evening. With inscription, red ribbon and all it was given a place of honour on the wall behind his desk in the office. There it collected dust until Braunthal's retirement in 1957.

Fourteen years were left to Braunthal after his retirement to write a three-volume history of the Socialist International. To do this in the final stage of his life had been his great wish. He was actually always happiest in delving into books and in writing.

Until 1963 when I retired, two other secretaries served the International (now the title is General Secretary). First there was Bjarne Braatoj, a Norwegian, also once on the staff of the Labour and Socialist International. From the start, there was an easy understanding between us. Before long we were friends who trusted each other absolutely. In his short period of office (he died after less than a year) he tried to give the International the "modern face" he thought it needed. Braatoj's death was a great loss for me personally. I believe it was a loss for the International as a whole.

Unhappily, on the other hand, my relations with his successor, Albert Carthy, formerly a staff member of the British TUC, were tense and difficult from the start (he retired in 1969). I feel that the less is said about this dismal subject the better. What mattered to me most was my work and in this I had the support of colleagues and friends everywhere.

During nearly all of the thirteen years I worked for the Socialist International I was Editor of *SII* and rapporteur for meetings and conferences. I appreciated the unique opportunity this gave me to watch closely all that happened in the Labour and Socialist movement throughout the world. In producing with considerable effort so much material over many years I was sustained by the hope that future historians of the International would find it useful. Meeting many interesting personalities also added to the interest of my work. I regret not having found a way of making more of them come alive in these pages.

An attempt to analyse developments in the International in the years when I was part of it would go beyond the framework set for these personal memoirs. I therefore limit myself in concluding this chapter to a few general comments. Despite the limitations for which the International had been rightly or wrongly blamed, I never ceased to assign considerable importance to it. The very fact that it has provided regular opportunities for free contact, exchanges of views and cooperation at all levels on vital issues, gives it a unique position among the political forces in the world. The existing opportunities have not always been sufficiently utilised. The task of making the International, despite limited possibilities, an effective instrument under the leadership it needs has certainly not received high enough priority. In this I see a great challenge for the future.

In addition to my previous tasks in the International—undertaken on a part-time basis—I took on a new responsibility in 1954: that of international women's secretary described in the next chapter. As women's activities expanded, the job became very full-time indeed. But this was not officially recognised by the Bureau of the International until 1962 when I was relieved of my editing function. With becoming women's secretary, my scope for an independent development of activities greatly increased.

XV

Women's Secretary

If I had been told in my youth that one day I would be a women's organiser I would just have laughed. It continued to look most unlikely for a long time. Yet it happened in the final stage of my professional life. From 1954 to 1963, I was women's secretary of the Socialist International. If I add the years of voluntary work after 1963, I can look back on more than two decades in which a great deal of my time was devoted to women's activities.

My interest in the women's cause started long before I became active in public life. It found expression even in my childhood dream of going to India to help women there to obtain the medical attention denied to them because of prejudice. In preparing myself for university studies not envisaged by my parents I took steps towards my own emancipation. I responded readily to women leaders and their visions of women's rôle in society. As my awareness of being a socialist deepened, the belief in sex equality became an integral part of my philosophy of life. The fight for this belief was but one aspect of the fight against injustice. There was a class angle to this question, too. The position of the poorer, less educated women was far worse than that of the economically and educationally privileged. I realised, too, that the franchise was no guarantee of economic and social equality, either for men or women.

However deeply I felt committed to the principle of women's equality, women's organisations did not appeal to me for a long time. As a young woman I wanted to have the company of men and the stimulus that comes from joint efforts with them. Moreover, in the troubled circumstances of Weimar Germany it seemed essential not to divert men's and women's energies into separate channels, but to co-operate in endeavours to save society from the tightening grip of nationalist reaction and, soon, the fascist threat. The threat of Hitler concerned women directly. The Nazis denied them equal rights with a fanatical zeal.

My personal circumstances did not make me want to join a women's group either. I did not experience any blatant discrimination as a woman. My parents did not put any obstacles in my way when I was determined to study; on the contrary, they helped me. The doors of the university stood open to me. Women gained political rights just as I became old enough to vote. Many women tend towards associations of their own sex when they feel restricted under an inadequate family and social structure imposed on them. I suffered no restrictions on that ground.

Leaving aside my personal situation, I realised of course, and wrote articles about the question, that there were unresolved women's questions. From my own experience, I knew that a special approach to women could be useful in adult education. For I taught groups of women at my place of work and in trade unions. The abortion law, for whose abolition I campaigned, affected women in the first place. From my intimate contact with working class families I knew only too well that they were the ones to suffer directly from Paragraph 218. It was natural, therefore, that organisations such as the "League for the Protection of Mothers" should recruit women in particular. But in my speeches I always stressed that family planning through contraception must be preferred to abortion with its risks for women.

My experiences in Britain after 1933 made me realise the useful role of many women's organisations. They were fulfilling an educational rather than a merely charitable function, especially among educationally disadvantaged women who would rarely take an interest beyond their own family circle without the help of a women's group. The training of women for responsibility in party, trade unions and co-operatives—often through women's sections or guilds—was a vital factor in British public life, especially in local government.

My life in Britain affected my attitude in more than one way. I saw that co-operation was possible and useful even among women belonging to different political camps, for instance, on occasions in Parliament. I was impressed by the political climate which left room for such flexibility. A refusal on rigid doctrinal grounds ever to co-operate with "bourgeois" women's groups persisted in many continental countries well into the post-war years. Even in Britain, the women of the Labour movement joined the National Council of Women at a relatively late stage.

While, gradually, I acquired a better understanding of the arguments in favour of separate women's organisations I was aware of a danger to be guarded against. Their advancement, their effective partnership with men can be retarded by their being isolated too much, or for too long, in sex-based groups. I remember being struck by an argument used by the Swedish leading woman, Alva Myrdal, when I first met her. She stressed that many men who were basically opponents of women's equality liked to see them confined to their own little corner in society, if no longer to their homes. It is true that "Women's Lib", though keen on separate women's groups, is not content to be confined to any corner, but thrives on confrontation and publicity. Pressure group tactics can indeed be effective in bringing to the fore demands the realisation of which is overdue. The Congress of the Socialist International had to be prompted by its women's council before it at last in 1972 publicly recognised the urgency of such demands, neglected even within the movement itself. My reservations about Women's Lib concern its tactics, which are apt to jeopardise the partnership between men and women which is necessary for progress in society, in both developed and developing countries. For the latter, moreover, its message is often practically irrelevant. It emphasises overmuch the problems which are acute in the industrialised world.

A job in women's activities had not been my aim, but when I accepted it in 1954 my attitude was wholly positive. At international level in particular, I saw prospects of important development.

My work since 1950 had brought me into contact with many leading women from different member parties. They were dissatisfied with the International's Women's Committee revived soon after the war. As rapporteur, I had attended the early women's conferences and knew how miserable the situation was. At the suggestion of delegates from various countries, Julius Braunthal asked me whether I would agree to serve as women's secretary. Since I was familiar with the work of the entire International, he thought, I would have no difficulty in integrating women's activities into its framework. I agreed, and in 1955 I was formally elected as secretary by the international conference in London.

It was virtually a new start, for which initiative and perseverance were needed. The confidence placed in me by women I had come to like and respect was very encouraging. With a certain pride I began to draw two million politically organised women, through their representatives, into expanding international co-operation.

Some of the previous patterns were maintained, but there were also new ventures. Regular programmes included meetings, seminars, summer schools, conferences, messages, reports, a monthly bulletin, frontier rallies. A pamphlet (*Labour Women of the World*) was prepared for the fiftieth anniversary of the Women's International in 1957, impressively celebrated in Vienna. The most urgent need, however, was for a "new look" to be given to our organisational framework. A more independent structure was required instead of a mere committee of the International, especially for our work in the UN and its specialised agencies. In 1955 a statute, rules of procedure and a new name were adopted: the International Council of Social Democratic Women was born (ICSDW). For the sake of brevity I shall refer to "we" where this seems sensible.

Our struggle for "getting in" as a recognised non-governmental organisation (NGO) then began. It lasted several years. Opposition came from the communist side, but also from others who disliked socialist organisations. Finally we climbed up to the desired category B in the UN Economic and Social Council with its Commission on the Status of Women and UNESCO. Our admission to the desired category B corresponded to our size and activities.

We almost missed our chance of obtaining the change from C to B at UNESCO in 1962. What happened was significant. One day in Paris, Pippa Harris of UNESCO's Education Department mentioned in a personal talk with Mary Sutherland, then our Chairman, and me that a general survey and revision of NGO categories was in progress, in fact nearly completed. We were shocked because we had heard nothing about it—through whose fault we never found out. Luckily we had not missed the date set for the replies to the questionnaires. An interview was hastily arranged with the responsible official. We tried to impress him by skilful mention of the fact that Mary had for years been the British Government's delegate to the Commission on the Status of Women. We knew that in the UN NGOs were considered but poor relations in comparison to the all-important governments. We were admitted to category B, whether due to our Paris interview or our good record fully set out in our application I do not know.

Difficulties often arose in dealings with the large UN bodies with their top-heavy bureaucracy. I had my share of headaches. In 1963, for instance, I applied to UNESCO for a grant to cover some overseas fares for our Seminar at Saltsjöbaden in Sweden. Through the grape-vine I learned that our request was being favourably considered. But the confirmation in the form of a long, complicated "contract" reached me only when the would-be beneficiaries of this money were on their way from three continents. I had had to accept the financial responsibility in my personal capacity if I was not to lose valuable participants. Not being a bureaucrat, I was willing to accept such a risk.

Soon after the war, international development aid became an important issue, also within the Socialist International. What contribution could we, as a Women's Council, make in this field? Hardly anything was then known about women's position in most of the newly emerging countries. It fell to me to find out and suggest ways of approach and co-operation, a pioneering task which was challenging but exciting. In seeking contacts I could rely only to a limited extent on parties connected with the International. In Asia this looked hopeful in the fifties, and the first delegation of eight women invited for a study visit in 1959 came from Asia. Our affiliates in the four Nordic countries sponsored the visit.

As for Africa, our decision to send a NGO representative to the UN seminar in Addis Ababa in 1960 proved decisive. There, women of the "dark" continent emerged for the first time on an international platform. I was not present but I sensed the tremendous impression this historic occasion made all over the world. Our representative was Mina Ben Zvi from Israel. Her visit to Africa and the support from Golda Meir, then Israel's foreign minister, and Inga Thorsson of Sweden, for a time head of the UN's Division for Social Development, led in 1961 to the establishment of the Mount Carmel Centre in Haifa for the training of women from developing countries for community services. The Centre developed into a unique educational institution, and is an example of international, in particular Israeli–Swedish, co-operation on governmental as well as non-governmental level.

From the start, the ICSDW and many of its affiliates supported the Centre's activities, mainly through scholarships. This accorded with our decision of 1955 to seek co-operation with women in developing countries, especially in the field of education. For there the neglects of the past seemed worst and the needs of the future most pressing. Our decision to make our contribution to development aid in this way meant that it was not confined to a party basis. This was a radically new departure, and I worked hard to win understanding for it. It was necessary to extend the vision of our members in the economically more developed countries. I utilised every opportunity in every country, in Britain too, to this end.

In human terms, my close and untroubled association with the dozen or more members of our Working Committee, which was responsible for planning and coordinating our work, made these years very rewarding for me. I worked happily under—or rather with—three Chairmen of the ICSDW: for three years Nina Andersen, Danish Social Democratic women's secretary, a member of Parliament, leader in the Danish section of UNICEF; for two years the late Mary Sutherland, Chief Woman Officer of the British Labour Party; and for two years Rita de Bruyn Ouboter, the Dutch Labour Party's women's secretary, a biologist by profession before taking up politics. These were three outstanding personalities, intelligent and generous, all with a sense of humour, which eased difficulties and made for good companionship. They possessed a wealth of knowledge and experience in the field I had entered actively at a fairly late stage, and I was always able to consult them and benefit by their advice. I had good relations also with many outside the Working Committee, for example my fellow members on a three-month mission to Asia in my final year as secretary.

The session of the ICSDW conference in Amsterdam in 1963 at which I took my leave was a very moving occasion. Tears were in my eyes (unusual for me) and, as I noticed, in those of others. Many of the friendships established in the course of joint endeavours have endured and co-operation for common purposes has continued to the present day.

XVI

Retirement and Self-chosen Missions

My Swedish friend Anna Rudling, who was with me on our strenuous tour of Asian countries in 1962–1963, reported on our return, using a Swedish term, that I had been *den starka hästen* (the strong horse). The label stuck. What was the strong horse going to do with her years of retirement?

The problems which hit many people at that stage did not affect me when my turn came in 1963. I was in good health and free from financial worries, thanks to compensation I was receiving from Germany for lost income during the Hitler period. I was not lonely either, living in a harmonious family unit and in contact with many friends at home and abroad. I knew beforehand that my retirement would be an active one. I wanted to see more of the world, while making myself useful.

There had to be some psychological adaptation. Retirement meant to leave the pressures of time-tables, deadlines and regular commitments, and to start a life of freer choices. Activities now depended on my own decisions, even those still connected with the ICSDW, such as attendance at UN or UNESCO meetings or writing for the Council's Bulletin. To ease the transition, I went away from London for the first few months. Invitations from the West Indies and some Latin American countries led to my first "self-chosen mission".

Soon a certain pattern developed. Larger tours in Latin America, the West Indies, the Middle East, Asia and Africa, lasting between two and five months, formed the centre pieces. Usually they were preceded by considerable preparations, in one case even the learning of Spanish, for me a new language. Usually once a year I visited Israel, which enabled me to participate in the work of the Mount Carmel Centre, as rapporteur, lecturer, resource person or just as guest visitor. I became more and more identified with this work. Often I met Mount Carmel participants again in their home settings in Africa or Asia. Nearly all of them were putting to practical use what they had learned in Israel.

Visits to Western Europe for conferences or lecture tours were part of the ordinary run of things, as they had been before. Less ordinary were visits to Eastern Europe. When a certain relaxation in East–West relations began, especially when West Germany's *Ostpolitik* was launched, I thought the time had come for me to try to take up some relations with people behind the Iron Curtain, but I took every possible care to avoid serving anybody's propaganda purposes. I was able to do so since I was now in a rather independent position. I was familiar enough with the situation in countries like Poland, past and present, not to take official statements at their face value. Many democratic socialists unfortunately know too little or are too uncertain of their own fundamental beliefs to argue effectively with communists or even win their respect. I found some communists with whom I could be frank in personal talks. Some were evidently longing for more honest relations with us in the West, free from Soviet Russian control. Some, after a certain mutual trust had miraculously been established, would advise me in confidence whom to trust and with whom to be careful. We had discussions on such questions as the future of the satellite states and the possibility of their advancing towards a democratic society—they would say "advance towards a humanised communism". Such talks were very moving experiences.

In most years of my retirement, I spent nearly a total of six months away from London. At home, articles, reports, editing, translating and an extensive correspondence have kept me busy. Other preoccupations have included work as trustee and secretary for two foundations: the Nora Henry Trust, which provides grants for educationally underprivileged people, especially of developing countries, and—linked with an earlier period in my life—the Society for the Furtherance of Critical Philosophy, which aims to promote interest in Leonard Nelson's philosophy in the English-speaking world.

Recently I became a governor of a comprehensive secondary school at Hampstead. I enjoy being in touch with modern educational trends and with the very young. Meeting Rene's students keeps me in contact with the student generations. Domestic duties have provided a healthy counter-balance to intellectual pursuits. Late in life I developed a liking for cooking. With a constant flow of visitors to our home, I have ample opportunity to satisfy this interest.

As before, so after my retirement I spent holidays frequently at Alforno in the Tessin in the South of Switzerland, often with friends whom I invited. Usually one would meet friends there in any case. Alforno is a holiday home in the mountains built during the war by René and Hanna Bertholet for their friends who after the war would need a place for rest, study or discussion. The beautiful scenery and the congenial atmosphere attracted me again and again. Mascha Oettli has done so much to maintain this atmosphere. With Mascha I have been closely linked since the days when she was a student at the *Walkemühle;* we co-operated especially while she was women's secretary of the Swiss Social Democratic Party.

Thus I did have the active retirement envisaged. Yet life is too short, I found, and the world too big for me. At the end I am still left with unfulfilled wishes and unrealised ambitions. A glance at the map (see Plates) shows that I have not done badly. All the countries of which I have first-hand knowledge are marked. Some I have visited only once or twice, others more often, and in some I have lived for long periods. On grounds of health I recently slowed down my pace considerably, but have not yet given up travel altogether.

My "missions," such an important part of this period, deserve a more detailed account. How did I choose the countries for an overseas tour? How were my programmes arranged? There were always people who urged me to come and promised to help with a useful programme, useful to the people and organisations with whom I was connected: political parties, trade unions, educational institutions, in particular women's groups. Often suggestions came from participants at Mount Carmel Centre. Eagerly they promised to look after me if only I would come! Most proved as good as their word. Looking back I am really amazed how easily things took shape, how many people were willing to co-operate: friends working at various embassies, especially Israelis, representatives of international aid agencies, and a host of others.

The insight into problems and the contacts I gained have deepened my understanding of many parts of the world in a way books and statistics could never have done. I thought for example I knew much about Indian poverty, but discovered in India how superficial my knowledge was. In Bombay 500,000 people are "pavement dwellers" (the official term used) who sleep every night in the streets—the cold print becomes a reality when you actually see them lying there in street after street. A social worker took me to one-room slum dwellings each shared by up to eight families and also serving as a work shop, with a few watertaps and toilets on landings for hundreds of people. Even a pavement dweller's existence might be preferable, I thought. On the last evening we spent in Bombay in 1962, Anna Rudling, Lea Brakin and I were invited to dinner by the Editor of the *Times of India.* He asked us to let him have a piece by next morning on our impressions of Bombay with suggestions for what the City Council could do. Dead tired and hot we sat up in our beds at midnight, searching for something to say. We could not possibly let the man down. I remember the proposal Anna finally put down: the City Council should clean the streets not only in the mornings, but once more before nightfall. For the sleepers, as we had noticed, did not only occupy the pavements but also the middle of the roads where during the day cars, horses and cows had passed.

In Delhi, nights in January were bitterly cold. To go to appointments I often took a taxi outside the little Indian hotel where I stayed. Invariably a huddled figure wrapped in rags and newspapers who had been sheltering in the taxi would get out. Climbing the stairs to a meeting place in Old Delhi I stumbled over mothers with babies, sheltering in corners—a very usual sight. Was there any progress in women's conditions, I often wondered. I asked Indira Gandhi, who gave me an interview in the palace where she then still lived with her father Nehru, to whom I was also introduced. She said: "When I was a young girl and accompanied my father on his propaganda tours of villages, many women were unable to come to our meetings simply because they had no saris to wear. Today even the poorest woman has a sari or two." She added: "Many women attend political meetings nowadays and, of course, go to the polls."

Poverty in Africa was shocking too, especially in some parts such as the dry north of Upper Volta, where I saw malnutrition most clearly written in the faces of children who are always hungry. Yet that day was the Muslim holiday Ramadan, and one of the village elders quickly wrung the neck of a chicken when our cars stopped for the goodbye, so that the guest could have the customary gift. Under a UNESCO project the women in that area had been brought together for the first time in a community effort. One of the improvements under the project was a hygienic maternity hut. This was awaiting its first occupants.

Stark poverty was often matched by points of progress. Among my friends there were many social workers who had started improvement programmes, with or without government help: a Montessori kindergarten in the midst of a slum; a co-operative workshop where women could earn some much-needed supplement to the family income; an arts and crafts centre where villagers brought articles they had made at home for sale; family planning centres started by women's groups, unaided at a time when governments were far from ready to take action in this field. When I visited these social workers in their homes, I was again and again struck by the lack of even elementary facilities. How easy it was for us in Europe to complain when they did not send reports and accounts regularly! Seeing their home surroundings, I felt ashamed about our expectations.

In Latin America, so statistics tell us, poverty is less extensive than in Asia and Africa. The conditions for example in the mountainous areas of

Peru where the Amer-Indians live are appalling enough. Once I visited a
rural market, and there was a sudden downpour of rain. I was led into one
of the houses; it was worse than a pig sty. I noticed that most women who
did the walking and carrying on market day went barefoot, while the
men, even the bigger boys, would wear sandals. Evidently women were not
considered worth spending scarce money on.

The sight of women in Africa carrying the heaviest burdens shocked me
many a time. I needed only to look around to see evidence of their
drudgery—"they are used to it" was the standard comment. Unforgettable
the old shrivelled woman in Togo on her way to the market, with her
breasts hanging down almost to her knees, carrying on her head a live pig
without even the wooden frame in which another one carried a calf. Even
the men now admit that the younger women will opt out of their inhuman
burdens when they can. They move to the towns even when there is little
prospect of work there, creating increasing urban problems.

I had opportunities in Africa to see something of tribal customs which
still have a considerable hold over people. I remember two memorable
days during a stay in Sierra Leone which I spent at the home of a
paramount chief, a woman I had met at the Mount Carmel Centre. There
she used to introduce herself by saying: "I am the ruler of 30,000 people".
With her turban she was a truly majestic figure. Her chiefdom was a few
hours' drive by car from Freetown. What a reception I had! I had never
dreamt of being carried in a procession, yet that is what happened, in a
long palanquin, with four strong men holding up the poles. From the
chief's house to the village hall, the procession became longer and longer,
people joining all along the way, the school children fanning me with their
school books—it was terribly hot. We passed the secondary school, of
which the people are very proud, for they built it with their own hands.
But the paramount chief had taken the initiative, secured support from the
women's federation whose President she was at that time, and found
foreign volunteers as teachers.

In the crowded hall, the people were delighted to hear my account of
how I had met their "Madam" (as they called her), and what she had then
told me about the 30,000 people in her chiefdom. And now I had come to
see for myself. At night, the people came to dance for hours to several
drums on the lawn outside the chief's house, overlooking the cliffs and the
sea. The chief joined in merrily. Next day when I went back to Freetown
with her in her car, she told me about her life and her functions. Officially
she no longer wielded any judiciary powers but many still came to her for
judgment. Everywhere the people rushed out to greet their Madam. I
composed my thank you letter in rhymes, as I often did after a memorable
experience. I cite these verses:

To my friend, the Paramount Chief Madam Honoria Bailor Caulker

It was like a dream
Or so it would seem
That again we should meet
It was a rare treat.

On Israel's shore
We had met before
And when we parted
A friendship had started.

So I heeded your call
To see you, and all
Shenge's people as well
Now a tale I can tell.

Of Shenge, its school,
Built with many a tool
By the people's hand
And not built on sand.

Of the honour they did
Man, woman and kid
At the chief's request
To me as her guest.

I was carried along
By four men strong
With girls by my side,
What a strange ride.

The women did dance
Not missing a chance
Along all the way
Where the village hall lay.

And every one came
Who was not lame
To hear my brief
And their Paramount Chief.

I have rarely seen
An audience so keen
So ready for fun
Under Africa's sun.

At night just the same
When many came
To drums they did bring
To dance and to sing.

Midnight had passed
When the very last
Still full of zest
Went home to rest

From fun and laughter.
But soon thereafter
Broke loose the storm
True to tropical form.

Shenge will stay
For ever, I say,
Unique in its kind
Engraved in my mind.

Though we must part
With all my heart
My thanks I send
To you, dear friend.

Did I make myself useful as I had hoped I would? The response I had seemed to vindicate that hope. I believe that I made people feel they belonged to a wider community which shared problems and aspirations, a feeling which can inspire and encourage. Observing and learning about local problems, I was able to make suggestions and extend advice on dozens of matters of which I would not have known otherwise. The wider the range of my knowledge, the better I was able to do so.

After my four weeks in Trinidad in 1963–1964 as the guest of the Women's League of the People's National Movement (the ruling party) Isabel Teshea, its Chairman–Minister of Health and Housing, later Ambassador in Addis Ababa, then Guyana–asked me for a personal report so that she and the League might benefit by my observations. She appreciated the frankness of my comments, which was very gratifying; a lasting friendship was formed. I had drawn her attention, for example, to her way of referring to "our" or "this country's" Christian faith or culture, when nearly 40 per cent of the population were of Indian origin and certainly not Christians.

Did everything always go smoothly? Have I given too rosy a picture? Of course, there were difficulties: delays in obtaining visas, misunderstandings about arrangements, mosquito bites, an accident when I fell down some stone stairs, and had to be rushed to hospital, and, most embarrassing of all, as I was just moving on to another country, had a disfigured face. More important still were problems in communicating, even in relations with very good friends. No wonder, when constantly wide gaps between cultures have to be bridged.

Mercedes Fermin was my guide in Venezuela, a wonderful inventive guide. I had much in common with her politically because her experiences in the long fight against the dictator, Juan Vicente Gomes, were very similar to mine in the struggle against the Nazis. Yet there were tensions. She was vexed by my impatience and unhappiness about delays and unpunctuality, hers and that of others. She simply hated my frequent glances at my watch. "Why don't you try to adapt to our way of life when you are here?" she once burst out. She herself had come to the conclusion that a watch was a tyrant, and refused to wear one. However, there were other irritants in her life which explained why, for instance, she failed to telephone me despite her promise to do so. She taught geography at the Caracas University, which, at that time, was controlled by the communists who intimidated the staff, besides hiding guerilla terrorists and weapons on the campus where the police were not allowed to enter. Because Mercedes was not on their side, the communists prevented her from telephoning; they saw to it that she never got an outside line.

When I was staying with our "adopted" Jonn's family in Ghana, his father once asked me, somewhat bewildered: "I have been watching you now for a few weeks and gone around with you to many places. But I still do not know what makes you tick." I tried to explain, but Geormbeeyi found it difficult to appreciate the reasons why I should spend my own money on fares and earn nothing for my efforts. Why, he wondered, at my age was I going to places where I suffered from the heat? Why did I travel to remote rural areas in uncomfortable buses on bad roads? Why did I address meetings of ordinary women often badly attended? Why did I chase after addresses of people I wanted to contact (discovering how little use a telephone directory could be or how out-of-date a map of the city)? Geormbeeyi is a well educated man, thanks to his innate ability, his drive and the encouragement he received from his father, a cocoa farmer with many children from his four wives, who stood up for Geormbeeyi when the village elders wanted him to start working on the communal land instead of continuing his education. Still, being a fairly typical African man, he found my keen interest in the conditions and fate of women strange. He was not at home in the world of women's concerns in which he saw me moving with such ease, a world in which, he noticed, a natural community of the like-minded exists everywhere. I remember his remark after our visit to Annie Jiagge, the Ghanaian judge and one of the foremost African women leaders, that he "had felt at sea". The same night, at a party, I caused great amusement among the African men present when I suggested offhand that Ghana would do well with Annie as President or Prime Minister.

A few years later, in International Women's Year and following suggestions from the UN, the Ghanaian Government set up a National Council on Women and Development with the aim of raising the standard of living of women on a broad national basis. Among its twenty members four are men, and Geormbeeyi is one of them. He wrote to me that he was appointed on the basis of the contribution he was expected to make, and he added: "I can't discount your personal influence and inspiration in my nature and fabric!"

Difficulties in communication—how many examples I could mention! All of them interesting and instructive, but one more may suffice. It is from Japan. I was to address a meeting of fishermen on the East Coast who were working on a co-operative basis, supporters of the Socialist Party at election time. Manae Kubota, who had become a close friend when she was Rene's student at Hillcroft College, acted as my interpreter. When we arrived, I was told that my audience wanted me to talk about the fishing industry in England. I had to confess my ignorance (as a vegetarian I don't even eat fish) and chose another topic: relations between the sexes, marriage customs and the like, comparing Japanese with British customs. Manae's apparently charming translation evoked many laughs, and they took it all in goodhumouredly. But when question time came, every single question was about fish. In the end I just shrugged my shoulders and laughed, and everybody joined in. They would not believe that an intelligent person, so widely travelled, could be so ignorant about a subject of the greatest importance.

After the meeting, we went out to meet the wives who were just returning from their day's work at the seaweed beds (seaweed is a Japanese delicacy) nearby. At once we got into a lively conversation about their work, their households, their children and how they combined it all—a popular theme among women all over the world. In Japan, more than anywhere else, I found it was infinitely easier to establish contact with women than with men. Women seemed to have been so much more affected by the post-war winds of change.

In most countries I presented something of a puzzle to some women, even among those active at local, regional, national and international levels. They were anxious to know precisely under whose auspices I had come, in other words, who had paid my ticket and was covering other expenses. Perhaps they suspected hidden political motives? This seemed sometimes the case with women who had to account to their governments for their relations with me. Mostly, however, they were simply puzzled about some one keen enough to pay her own expenses in the service of a cause, also for their sake, as it were, which was a novelty for them.

Through articles, reports and lectures I tried to share my experiences with others as far as possible. More recently I started writing books, these memoirs being the second one. The first was on the Mount Carmel Centre, published early in 1974 under the title *For Community Service—the Mount Carmel Experiment* by Blackwell, Oxford.

The idea to write the first was born in a talk with Mina Ben Zvi, director of the Centre, when I joined her in Holland for a day in 1972. We sat in the charming garden of Rita de Bruyn's home at Huizen, a converted fisherman's cottage where I have often been a guest. We were able to talk quietly for hours, which is rarely possible in Israel where Mina is absorbed in her very busy life. Our talk turned to the documents accumulating at the Centre which embodied much information and experience of general interest, particularly on the role of women in community development. We agreed that these duplicated papers in their bulky form were of little use. "You write a book", Mina told me, "we will co-operate with you, but you must do it and find your own publisher." In her persuasive way, she encouraged me to accept the challenge. It was a challenge for me but I enjoyed the work in preparing the book and the warm response it evoked.

The human bonds which I have been able to establish throughout the world over so many years are a source of lasting personal satisfaction. Once I talked with a friend about my eightieth birthday, still a few years ahead. He asked me whom I would like to have around on that occasion. To his surprise I said: "All my daughters". He knew I had only one. So what did I mean? I meant women in that age group who were very close to me, as close as daughters. I was able to mention at once about a dozen names from my global kind of extended family. It gives me a good feeling to think of such a global birthday party although it will probably remain a dream.

Index